ThE OuteR DarknesS

Dominic Peloso

Dark Mountain Books

Copyright ©2024 Christopher Dominic Peloso

Cover Design and illustrations by Junnie Chup

All Rights Reserved. No part of this publication may be reproduced, stored in a retrieval system or transmitted, in any form or by any means, electronic, mechanical, photocopying, recording or otherwise, without prior written permission of the copyright holder.

Publisher's Note:
This is a work of fiction. Names, characters, places, and incidences are either the product of the author's imagination or are used fictitiously, and any resemblance to any actual person living or dead, organizations, events, existential catastrophes, biblically-accurate angels, rotating black holes, or locales is entirely coincidental.

ISBN: 978-1-931468-40-4
First Printing

(all of this is true)

Chapters:

The Girl	....	7
The Factory	....	33
The Park	....	63
The War	....	83
The Cathedral	....	107
The Novel	....	133
The Diner	....	151
The Barge	....	177
The Grave	....	199

1

He had reached that age where he knew more than a few suicides– friends, loved ones, relatives, and enemies who'd contemplated the one truly serious philosophical problem and concluded that life in this entropic city was simply not worth the trouble. The Protagonist walked down the streets at a brisk pace, though with no particular destination in mind. It was raining, or, more accurately, it had been raining up until a few minutes ago; and the sidewalk was stained dark and slick with water. Small droplets on his glasses turned the streetlights into astigmatic pinwheels in his eyes.

The Protagonist loitered at the deserted street corner, more out of social obligation than safety, and waited for the traffic light to change. Above him, the light was performing without an audience. He stood still for longer than he needed too, as the light went from green to red to green to red again. Not a single car bore witness to this series of events. He wondered if, were he not there himself, would the light continue its purposeless task deep into the evening? More broadly, if all humanity keeled over dead tonight from some plague or armageddon, how long would this light continue to carry out its assigned duty? Maintaining safety on a cold, dead world. Red to green to red to green. He made a mental note to come back someday when he wasn't here to see how the light reacted to his absence.

Bored with this thought, the Protagonist continued on his journey. It was only a few blocks later that he remembered he forgot to look whether the light was red or green at the specific moment he stepped into the street, and if he was thus now a scofflaw. He continued under an overpass beneath a highway. The cars on the road above rattled the steel beams violently as they sped to their mysterious destinations. A stream of water from a broken gutter splattered on the pavement below. Somewhere in the distance, he could hear the sound of lonely instrument playing a single, constant note that droned on and on ceaselessly.

The next block contained what appeared in the dim light to be a small, dark cemetery; although perhaps it was just an apartment complex, above which telephone poles and wires crisscrossed in a far more complex pattern than one would think would have been necessary. Above the sidewalk, a streetlight sputtered and dimmed randomly, giving the shadows in the graveyard the illusion of movement. The block after that was mostly small, single-family homes, dark and dead at this late hour, but lights and music emanated from what appeared to be a squat and flat-roofed local bar that stood at an intersection of two nameless streets. The Protagonist had never noticed this particular establishment, but he would be the first to admit that he was not the most observant person, and so it might very well have been there all along. No one had cared to make the bar's nondescript, brick exterior inviting to prospective patrons. The only indications that it was a public house at all were a single blinking neon sign that shone through a small window to advertise a brand of beer, and the muffled sounds of multiple conversations emanating from within, partially obscured by music. He stood outside for a few minutes debating with himself silently.

In the alleyway next to the squat and flat-roofed bar, he noticed a faint rummaging sound coming from inside a large trash bin. It was either a racoon or an Erelim, but the slight blue glow emanating from under the lid implied the latter. The alley smelt of old milk. Some hooligan had scrawled graffiti in dripping black paint on the wall of the building. It said quixotically,

"Do you know where you are?"

A drink would be nice, to calm his thoughts, but he worried about having to justify his intrusion to the regulars inside. He didn't want to actually talk to anyone. He simply wanted to be *near* people who were talking. To listen in. To feel included. To feel connected to something outside his own thoughts. But only in theory. Trying to make an actual connection with someone seemed too much work for this late in the evening, and was well outside his current abilities and desires. But he went in anyway, not wanting to loiter in the street and arouse suspicion. It might start raining again any minute.

The inside of the bar, like most bars of the city, was dark; lamps dimmed to a dull brown glow that was further obscured by a hardened crust of dust baked onto their shades of colored glass. On the walls, neon lights brightly advertised different brands of liquor, interspersed with an odd collection of flotsams that bore no discernable theme other than some unspecified sentimentality to the owner. The Protagonist half-heartedly looked around for anyone he knew, but no one seemed particularly familiar, at least not individually. In the aggregate, they at least seemed similar to people he was familiar with, and that was comfort enough for an evening like this. There was no one to greet him when he entered, but he lingered by the door for a few seconds anyway, as his eyes adjusted to the smoke. In the back, a few regulars hovered intently over a game of pool. The majority of tables and booths sat unoccupied, though several hosted groups of people in twos and threes, sometimes chatting, sometimes not. A number of unoccupied tables still had empty glasses on them, droplets of water from condensation slowing dripping onto the soiled paper napkins beneath. A television hung near the ceiling broadcasting a movie, soundless and unintelligible.

He removed his coat and hat and shook off the remnants of the rain. He smoothed the hair on his forehead with the back of his hand, and sat down on a black vinyl stool near the end of the bar. A piece of duct tape inelegantly repaired a large tear in the seat cushion. There was a bartender present, but all the way at the other end, half-obscured by steam pouring upwards from a dishwasher. The Protagonist waited patiently. Behind the bar was a mirror. He saw himself. "Is that really what I look like?" he thought. His reflection appeared old, older than he expected. The lighting was poor in here though, so perhaps his haggard visage was just a trick of the shadows.

It was only in the mirror that he observed the two women sitting nearby on the stools beside him. He hadn't noticed them when he sat down, and they hadn't noticed him either. He stared at them via the safety of the reflection for a few seconds. It was more comforting than looking at his own face. The two were engaged in an animated conversation. From their dress, one might surmise that the conversation was gossip about office interactions. He turned his ear and listened in passively. He could only comprehend every other word over the din of the background noise, and the names mentioned were meaningless to him, but it made him feel slightly less alone to hear words, even words not directed toward him.

He looked down at his shoes and waited for the bartender to notice him. His throat was dry. The music seemed to increase in volume and began to drown out any hope of comprehending any of the conversations around him. He was tired. His shoes were old, old and scuffed and covered with mud. The sound from the unseen speakers seemed to change from Top-40 into the rhythm of a beating heart. Was that just the sound of blood rushing through his arteries? He closed his eyes.

The thumping put him in a trance. He began to have a vision he'd had before. All of a sudden, he wasn't in a non-descript neighborhood bar, but was instead being lowered into a pit. The pit was smoky, and he could see the faint outline of a dragon, or some serpentine being of similar dimensions and ferocity, at the bottom, waiting for him. He was inexorably falling, but interminably slowly, as if he were tumbling downwards through a jar of lugubrious honey. The creature below was only half-aware of his presence.

"What'll it be?" said the bartender. The Protagonist looked up. "What are you drinking?" the man repeated with almost imperceptible annoyance. Disoriented, thankful to have been plucked out of the pit and returned to his seat, all he really desired was water. He ordered a glass of bourbon. The bartender chose not to ask his preferred brand, and wordlessly served him a short, thick glass with an inch of brownish liquid at the bottom. The Protagonist leaned down and breathed the acrid, burning scent into his sinuses. The sharpness began to bring him back into focus. He looked up to ask for some water, but the bartender had already moved elsewhere.

Still hunched over his glass, his eye caught the two women sitting to his left, they were staring at him. "Are you ok?" said one.

"Ok?" he repeated the question. "I suppose you mean in the specific sense, as in, 'am I sick to my stomach or feeling lightheaded,' and not in the broader, more philosophical sense. The answers to those two questions are quite different." He cleared his throat, straightened his posture, and let out a sigh. "But, for the present, I guess I am... ok." He half-smiled. "Just tired," he added after an uncomfortable pause. The women went back to their conversation. The Protagonist excused himself and went to the bathroom, leaving his drink at the bar.

"So anyway, I'm writing a novel," said Simone.

"You're writing a novel?" replied Hannah with a slight tone of surprise in her voice.

"Well, I'm just starting. I've never tried before. I guess I've been looking to take on a new project to help me find meaning and fulfilment in my life."

"Ugh. I wish I had the freedom to do that, but my family takes up so much of my time. Ok, I'll bite, what is it about?"

"Not sure yet, I'm using tone as a starting point instead of plot, so it's hard to say where it will take me. I'm letting the characters guide me where they want to go. But I am already worried about one thing."

"What's that?"

"Well, have you heard that theory about how almost no modern works of fiction have a scene in which two, named, female characters talk to each other about something other than a man?" said Simone.

"Is that true?" replied Hannah.

"I heard it's true. I guess so. I mean, I don't pay close attention to every single movie and book out there, but I can believe it. I want to make sure my novel passes that test."

"Ok, then do it."

"Yeah, you see, that's the problem. The book is told from the first person, and the main character is a guy, so there's no way to have a scene that he's not in. I mean, not without it seeming a little out of place and awkward."

"Have him go to the bathroom or something and have some ladies at the next table chit chat until he gets back."

"Talk about what though? It wouldn't be related to the plot."

"Does it have to forward the plot? I thought you were just looking to satisfy some arbitrary standard you'd set for yourself."

"Seems like it would be pretty obvious that I'm just doing it to pass some arbitrary standard unless it dovetails with and advances the rest of the story."

"That's an easy fix, just tell people you are writing a metaphysical novel. It's ok to do anything in metafiction these days as long as you tip off the reader that you are self-aware of what you are doing."

"When do I put the scene in?"

"Right in the beginning. Make it obvious from the start that your entire novel is self-aware of its inherent fictionality."

"hmmm..."

At that moment, the Protagonist returned from the bathroom. The two women continued their dialogue undisturbed, barely registering his return. He silently listened in to a mélange of conversations from several nearby tables. At regular intervals, anonymous people left the bar, only to be replaced by equally-anonymous people entering. Time elapsed slowly. The bartender poured several more drinks, and the Protagonist was even able to eventually get his glass of water. Every few minutes he could hear the clattered release of pool balls signifying that someone had won, someone had lost, and a new game had started.

Throughout this time, he didn't interact with any of the patrons, or do anything at all in particular. He remained quiet, even in his own thoughts. He let reality flow around him and through him with the tranquil awareness of vipassana. It was a pleasant respite for him to not dwell on his own thoughts for a while. He was lonely, but it wasn't a loneliness that could be solved with the pleasant yet innocuous banter found in a bar. It wasn't a loneliness that could be solved at all really. But for now at least, he could temporarily hold back the dread of his continued existence by consciously choosing to not dwell on it.

He closed his eyes and again breathed in the acrid fumes of alcohol emanating from his glass. When he opened his eyes, he noticed through the mirror that one of the women sitting next to him was leaving. She put on her coat and headed to the door. She did not acknowledge his presence as she left and the Protagonist chose to not speculate on her intended destination. He instead completely forgot her existence as soon as the door closed behind her, as if he were unaccustomed to object permanence. The woman who remained continued to nurse her drink quietly. He watched her through her reflection. Her posture was graceful, her dress stylish, but her face looked incurably sad and alone. She turned her head and caught his eye in the mirror.

"Did I overhear that you are writing a book?" he said to her, reactively.

"Yes." she replied. "I did brag about that, but honestly, I was mostly just trying to impress someone. I don't have much more than a vague outline and some ideas for a few sentences of snappy dialogue."

"Well, I've always felt that the key to being happy is to just keep yourself busy with unimportant nonsense and eventually you'll be dead. Writing books seems like a good project in that regard, even if it goes nowhere and you are just doing it to impress people you don't even care about. You should be commended and encouraged to continue."

"You don't think writing is a waste of time? I suspect you must also be a writer then?"

"No. No... Although I do sometimes wonder if I'm a fictional character in someone else's novel." He rubbed his eyes with his hand. "Maybe I'm a character in *your* novel, in which case it is vitally important that you finish this chapter. Otherwise I'll be stuck in this shabby neighborhood pub for eternity waiting for my next line."

"Well, I certainly couldn't subject you to a fate like that," she replied, with a chuckle. She introduced herself to him. They shook hands. They continued the conversation. They had several more drinks. They flirted awkwardly, and pitiably, but mostly apathetically, as it was apparent they were more attracted to the idea of simply not being alone than in any particular attribute of the other person. But it was what it was and they were both grateful for the attention, even if it was just unimportant nonsense.

Her eyes were half-closed by the time she whispered, "Do you want to get out of here?" He did. The Protagonist donned his now dry overcoat and helped her with her jacket. As they reached the street, she gestured, "my apartment is this way." They walked mostly in silence. In the bar their conversation had been muffled to the point of anonymity by the presence of other noises, but here on the empty and dimly-lit street, their inconsequential words would carry. Further awkward flirtation would seem embarrassing now that it might be overheard. He wondered if it might snow tonight. The air was beginning to acquire a crispness to it that he had to reach back into last winter's memory to recollect feeling. The pair walked several blocks through the streets, under streetlights and traffic lights, and crisscrossed overhead wires that pulsed with unknowable electrical signals being transmitted to and fro.

They reached a part of city where buildings were more than just squat and flat-roofed bars and small, unlit houses. Apartments and offices rose overhead like stirring giants. They were not particularly high, just five or six stories at most, but old, almost impossibly old, and covered with patches of the thick, black soot that betrayed their advanced age. Several still had lights burning in a few of their windows. The pair continued down the street until a body suddenly fell from the sky, landing with a wet thud on the pavement not fifteen feet in front of them. The Protagonist observed the crumpled corpse before them with little more than a sigh. A slow trickle of blood began to leak and wind its way past some litter into the gutter. "Hmmm." He mumbled, not having anything better to say. "They should be more careful when they do that, ...could have landed right on us." He looked up to see if there was any sign of where the person came from, but all seemed quiet and still on the balconies above.

"This is the third one I've seen just today," the woman remarked flatly.

"It's been happening more and more, everything just gets worse," he replied. The two stood around for a moment wondering if they should do something, but then a doorman came out of the building's entrance, walked over to the body, and waived them off. The Protagonist and the woman gingerly stepped around the scene and the puddle of blood and left the doorman to his grim task as he returned to the building to retrieve a mop.

The woman's residence was only a block further on. She fumbled with her keys for a second, and slid open the half-rusted gate that guarded the main entrance. Inside, the hallway was dark, but as the door closed behind them some overhead fluorescent bulbs sputtered to life with an almost imperceptible hum. The lobby floor was a checkerboard of white and black tiles, several cracked. The once-white walls were yellowed with age. Fixtures were in an art deco style that in the distant past was probably considered quite stylish and fashionable. "The elevator doesn't work," she said. "It hasn't worked for a long time now." She followed up with, "The super said that an Erelim made off with some irreplaceable part. I don't know." But she noted that she was only on the third floor. The stairwell echoed loudly as they made their way upstairs. The Protagonist observed that the marble steps all had deep indentations from repeated use. He wondered how many thousands of people over how many decades would have needed to traverse each landing to wear them away to that extent. He couldn't guess at an answer.

The pair then travelled through a long hallway filled with identical doors that led to presumably identical apartments. The

Protagonist heard muffled noises that might have been screams coming from behind one door, but he couldn't be sure. It might just have been a radio. She held the key ready in her hand by the time they reached her door. It swung open to reveal a cluttered yet welcoming apartment. There was a faint smell of incense or perfume still in the air. A dimmed lamp bathed the room in colored light. Dropping her purse by the door, she guided him to the couch and asked if he wanted a drink. He said yes reflexively, without giving the question consideration. In the kitchen she fumbled with the task of getting a cork out of a bottle.

"Do you do this often?" he called to her.

"This?" she replied, pouring some wine.

"Invite people to your apartment late at night?"

"Does it matter?" she said, sitting next to him and handing him a glass.

"No. I suppose it doesn't." He noticed that the glass wasn't a glass at all, but was a small canning jar, complete with threads at the rim for a lid. The wine was warm and sweeter than he preferred. He took a small sip and placed the jar on the table next to the sofa. She cuddled up next to him and threw her legs onto his lap. They avoided each other gaze for a

23

moment, when their eyes met, he attempted a smile.

She kissed him. Pulling away, she said drunkenly, "You smile like you're sad."

"Do I?"

"It's sort of cute," she replied. She leaned in and kissed him on his cheek. He could feel the heat of her breath against his neck. He could smell the scent of her hair. He put his arm around her. "That's nice," she whispered sleepily and nuzzled her forehead into his collar. "Aren't you glad you're not fictional?" she mumbled, making reference to his earlier comment from when they first met.

"I know you took it as a joke, and I guess I probably meant it that way, but I wasn't completely kidding about that, I'm really unsure what is real anymore." She chose not to reply. He sipped his too sweet wine and sighed. He continued, "it's like... I mean, take us, right now, sitting on this couch. This looks real right, this looks material, factual, tangible. You can touch it. We can touch each other." She put her hand on his forearm. "But this is only an instant, it's just *now*. There's nothing about us being here at this time that really informs where we were before, who we were before. I think I remember where I grew up, what school I went to, how I ended up on that street in front of the pub tonight, but am I right? And does it even matter? It's that everything that's ever happened before this instant is so intangible that it's impossible to actually say what is true and what is just our self-delusions."

She lurched forward so as to be on top of him and kissed him sloppily to shut him up. They fell into it, like a daydream, or a fever, lips and tongues entwined for a few moments as he fumbled with her sweater and she grinded her body against his as she held him down. Twice, they had to stop momentarily because her long hair had gotten entangled in his mouth, but they quickly came back together. With his hands around her waist, he could feel her chest expanding and contracting with each breath, could feel her aliveness. And she had chosen him, maybe not for any good reason, and maybe only for this single evening, but she had chosen him. For a second, he felt less alone.

"Hold on," she said suddenly. "I have to pee. I'll be right back." She jumped up off of him and disappeared behind a door, stumbling slightly as she went.

"...and if there's no real difference between what factually happened and what is just a fiction, then is it even possible to prove

I'm an actual, physical person and not just a fictional construct?" he mumbled under his breath after she left. The couch had a dark green, velvet cover that was soft, but slightly stained and somewhat disheveled. There were also several throw pillows which by now had been knocked to the floor. He picked them up and placed them back where they had started. He waited patiently for her return, sipping his cloying wine slowly. For a moment he wondered if the woman was real at all or just someone he'd made up in his head out of desperation. But he rejected this thought as his presence in this apartment wouldn't make sense if she was just a delusion, would it? She'd only been gone a minute, but he already missed the smell of her skin, and the weight of her body on his.

    Restless, he stood up and paced about the small apartment aimlessly exploring. There was a window that looked out onto the street below. The lights betrayed the presence of a fine mist in the air that might have been rain, or perhaps just a dense fog. Under the window was a radiator covered with a thick layer of paint that cracked and peeled in places, exposing several previous colors beneath. The furnishings were shoddy but functional; end tables covered with knickknacks, a pile of mismatched plates drying by the sink. Several photographs of people the Protagonist would never meet were affixed to the refrigerator door. An unremarkable landscape painting that was perhaps given to her by an artist friend, two vintage movie posters, a small mirror in a cheap, intricate frame. The floor was wood, faded and discolored in places, with a large, shag carpet covering most of it. He perused the titles of the books she kept on a shelf, to judge her tastes, and was surprised at the number he recognized (although had never gotten around to reading). He did the same with the records she had stacked next to the player. Her tastes here were clearly different than his, but he did come across one particularly obscure record that he had only ever seen once before, when a previous lover attempted to convince him of its merit. Strange to see it here as well.

As he looked around, he came to realize he wasn't in a particular apartment owned by a particular girl named Simone, but he was instead in an amalgamation of all the apartments, owned by all of the women he had ever been intimate with, all of the women who he had ever known, even possibly all the women he would never know. On a desk he recognized a flute that he was positive was the one played by a girl he dated who was in the school's marching band.

He recognized a pile of plums in a distinctively-chipped bowl that looked and smelled as delicious as the ones once picked from the backyard of someone he was serious about many years ago when he lived in a warmer climate. He noticed that there was now music playing; sounds of classic jazz that he first experienced late at night in the apartment of someone who turned out to be "just a friend" despite his best efforts.

    Above his head were small, white Christmas lights strung in the corners of the ceiling. Did he once help someone put those up? "I only ask because you are so much taller than me," he remembered hearing in a whisper. She still hadn't returned from the bathroom. He inspected several plants on the windowsill, half-dead from dehydration. He couldn't let them die again. He rinsed the dregs of wine out of his glass and filled it with water. The thirsty plants were grateful for the reprieve, but the Protagonist was sure he was only delaying the inevitable. He poured himself a little more of the wine and sat back on the velvet couch. He lifted a purple crystal off of the table and felt its weight in his hand. Had he held this particular stone before, or did an identical stone exist in all the apartments in the world? It seemed so similar.

    He was pretty sure he'd never had a serious romantic partner. He'd had flings of course, and one-night stands, and at least one ill-advised whirlwind affair. He was pretty sure of those. He had at numerous times spent months pining away for someone who would never return his affection, or spent months pushing away someone trying to get close to him because he knew he'd only end up hurting them in the end. He even had shared what he called 'love' with a partner, once, only to later realize he was unsure of what that term really meant. But he couldn't remember ever experiencing a soul mate; a person who understood him and whom he understood. He didn't even know if it was possible to really understand someone. The tragedy of existence is that everyone in the world only gets to experience reality from their one, single point of view. Sure, you could assume that other people thought like you and perceived the world like you, but there was no way to know that for certain. "Is what I call 'blue' also 'blue' to you, or do you see something totally different?" he thought. "Is what I call 'love' also 'love' to you, or do you feel something totally different?"

Eventually, tired of waiting, he went over to the closed door and peeked inside. The lights were on. The woman lay on her bed half-sideways, eyes closed, fast asleep. Her mouth was open and she was snoring daintily. He understood. It was late. He could go to her–climb into her bed and cover himself with her sheets and fall asleep in her arms. He did consider it. For the low cost of an awkward goodbye in the morning, he could revel in an entire evening of not being alone, of feeling skin on skin. But that would be the extent of it, wouldn't it? Skin on skin, not heart on heart, not soul on soul. Not love, not even lust, just a self-delusion shared by two people aching to fill a void that could never be filled authentically. He closed the door gently. He turned off the stereo and again washed out his glass in the sink, and washed out her glass as well, quietly putting them both on the rack to dry. He put on his shoes and coat. For a second he wondered if he should at least leave a note saying that he had a good time and offering his phone number if she wanted to do it again. But he realized that was pointless. He knew little about her life, and she knew even less about his. Nothing that had been said between them tonight hinted at the possibility of any deeper connection. She was sweet and pretty, and he was courteous and handsome, but there are millions of people in the world who are sweet and pretty and courteous and handsome. She would certainly not call. There was a decent chance she might not remember meeting him at all; her night being just a blur of strong cocktails and vague recollections of indistinct faces. He turned off the lights in the living room and let himself out, closing the door softly and carefully so as not to wake any at this late hour.

2

Somewhere in the distance, a church bell rang out several times. The Protagonist stepped over puddles and around the occasional pile of refuse strewn about in the gutters. The tall buildings soon fell away, almost as quickly as they had arisen. He passed through a neighborhood that appeared abandoned. The windows of the houses had been carelessly boarded up with plywood. The lawns a tangled mess of overgrown grasses, now dead and dying. Someone lived here once, raised children, talked sports and politics with neighbors across a wrought-iron fence, had barbeques and birthday parties and graduations and wakes. But no longer. Those people had grown up and moved away, or fell on hard times, or died. No one new had been willing to take their place, other than the wild plants and animals reclaiming their domain. He stopped for a second in an attempt to decipher some of the graffiti scrawled on a wall, but it was illegible.

He noticed a flickering of dim, orange light in a high window. It might have been a television, although there was no evidence that the building still had electricity. It might have been a fire some nameless tramp had set in order to keep warm. It might just have been a trick of the streetlights. He only spent a second considering the plight of whomever might still be up there in that leaky, drafty space. He walked on.

The next block he traversed was composed solely of a vast car park. There was a single streetlight overhead that illuminated no more than a small section of the lot. The rest lay in darkness. Only one car was resident at this hour. The Protagonist wondered if it was lonely. Was its owner working late? Perhaps out of town? His mind often went places he wished it wouldn't. He overthought everything. He found himself musing over the grim idea that maybe the owner had died suddenly, and the heirs hadn't yet found where the car was left last. More generally, he began to think about great tragedies; huge fires, mass shootings, buildings collapsing due to earthquake. When a calamity like that happens, presumably dozens of cars are abandoned for several blocks in all directions from the epicenter of the disaster. Was there a person whose job it was to drive around and identify them? Did each victim's family take on the task themselves? Eventually, they would probably all be towed away, if anyone cared enough to notice.

    On the corner after the car park there was a gas station. The lights were bright in the lanes and around the pumps. There was a small stand that sold drinks and snacks and windshield wiper fluid, but it was closed and dark and deserted at this late hour. A loudspeaker repeated an automated message, warning patrons to not accept offers from random strangers to help pump the gas for tips. It implied that malevolent drifters were afoot, and they would repay your kindness with treachery. There were no drivers at this hour to heed the mechanical warning. There were no malevolent drifters scurrying about in the shadows. The loudspeaker only preached to a swarm of large insects that flew in irregular circles around the lights above the station, and of course, to the Protagonist himself. He pushed his hands deep into his pockets to protect them from the cold.

Eventually, he found himself walking through an industrial area. This was a place that had some familiarity to him. He had worked here once, or at least he remembered he had worked here once. There, just down a side street lay the entrance to a large factory. He approached it– a solid brick structure that loomed over everything in its shadow. It was active, even at this late hour. Two smokestacks jutted from its roof like antenna and poured a thin orange haze into the sky that diffused and reflected the lights from below. The hum of the machinery inside, combined perhaps with the intermittent fog that rolled in, created the illusion that the building was breathing, albeit irregularly, like a giant injured beast wheezing its final breaths. A pipe that ran down the side of the structure had ruptured, and a black, viscous substance had been oozing down the wall for some time now. There was a fence surrounding the building, and a small gate that once had housed a security guard, but no one held that job these days. He ducked under the barrier and continued up to the front door.

If he had been asked, the Protagonist would have admitted that he was unsure why he went inside. Curiosity perhaps? To see what had become of this place in his long absence? A search for kinship perhaps? Maybe there was still a worker or two that would remember him from his time in the factory? A chance to talk about old times. It was summertime back then. Summertime and daylight. At least that's how he remembered it. Things seemed brighter in his memories, brighter and cleaner. The bricks of the outer walls hadn't had as much time to become weathered and stained black with soot. It was back in school, or more accurately, during a break from school, when he helped out here temporarily. Was it just a few weeks? The memories of youth are dim and distorted and stretched like light from a retreating star. His assignment had been simple enough. A pile of unstamped plastic lids in a bin to his left, a pile of stamped plastic lids in a bin to his right, and a machine that stamped lids in front of him. A small analog counter kept track of each stamp, 16... 17... 18... 507... 508... 509.... Every morning when he arrived, the counter was reset to zero. Every evening, a man would record how many lids had been stamped in a notebook. He never wrote down the correct number. "This counter must be broken," he told the Protagonist after his first day. "I've worked here 10 years and I never stamped as many lids in a day as this counter says. And I'm certainly much faster than you." The man wrote a much lower number in his notebook. "It doesn't matter anyway," he said, "you aren't looking to get promoted." Stamping was a mindless and monotonous and unfinishable task. At the time, the Protagonist liked the work for that exact reason. He could let his mind wander and puzzle out all sorts of philosophical problems in his head. The bin on the left would never be empty, no matter how many lids he stamped. The bin on the right would never be full. For that single summer at least, one must imagine the Protagonist happy.

He remembered the face of a coworker he'd fancied. He never knew her name, but she was pretty. Sometimes she would walk past his stamping machine on her way to or from some task, and their eyes would meet. A vending machine had stood in the breakroom in those days. It dispensed coffee and tea and cocoa and soup broth in little paper cups that fell down into position from some unseen location within the machine. Once, he arrived for his drink at the same time as the pretty girl. He graciously let her go first. She thanked him. That was the only conversation they ever had. He meant to talk to her again, he just never had the opportunity, or maybe he just never had the nerve. He was young and unsure of himself after all. On his final day at the factory at the very beginning of autumn, he followed her home, from a safe and respectful distance, hoping she would turn and notice him. He imagined witty things he would say to her once he caught her eye. She turned a corner and entered a building without once glancing back. He never saw her again. He forgot her soon after, the yearnings of passionate young men are fleeting and fickle. But on this night, her face once again flashed in his mind, and he wondered what had become of her.

  Why did he go inside the factory on this cold night? Boredom was the most likely answer. Boredom and a subconscious desire to warm himself on a chill evening. The entrance seemed inviting, in that a bright light streamed out from its glass doors, making it appear lively and inhabited compared to the otherwise dark and desolate street. However, the lobby of the building turned out to be completely empty. There was a reception desk, but it was unoccupied. There were a few couches and chairs, of a now-outdated style, scattered about, along with a few artificial plants. On a scratched, wooden table brochures related to the factory's products lay strewn about. He picked one up. The paper was dry and slightly yellowed at its edges, betraying the fact that it had rested on the table, undisturbed, for a long time. Its absence left a perfectly rectangular ghost of cleanliness in the light coating of dust on the table's surface. The brochure's cover prominently displayed a photograph of several attractive models who had been dressed up in the uniforms of the company's regular employees. The wide, bright smiles they wore were utterly dissimilar to the expressions of any co-workers the Protagonist could remember. He placed the brochure back on the table without opening it.

He proceeded through an unmarked door that led into the non-public area, and soon found himself in a changing room. Dozens of metal lockers painted in peeling beige paint decorated one wall. They were all open and empty. A union poster opposite from the lockers stated in big bold letters, "We are all in this together!" floating above the heads of several models who had been dressed up to look like proud union members. The Protagonist sat on the bench used for lacing up work boots and put his head in his hands. He was tired. With eyes closed, he listened to the familiar hum of the factory floor and imagined it full of people and life and energy. He imagined the past, and the faces of those he worked with. He could no longer remember any of their names, but he was sure he would as soon as he saw someone familiar. He crossed the changing room and entered the factory floor. On a rack by the door were some hard hats, and he donned one instinctively. All around him conveyor belts whirred and spun, moving half-finished products from one assembly station to the next with almost impossible alacrity and efficiency. Man-sized robotic arms carefully assembled, boxed, and wrapped the completed products for shipment. However, the floor was devoid of biological life. The Protagonist was the only living being there. He climbed the stairs up onto the grated balcony that ringed the production floor. From this higher vantage point, he could see and appreciate the intricate ballet of the machines. Everything was coordinated perfectly and with maximum efficiency. Next to him, on the wall, was a large red button with the words "emergency shutoff" above it. Below that was a disused first-aid kit and fire extinguisher. Over to one side of the factory floor he could see a machine stamping plastic lids and placing them into a bin to its right. He wondered if the counter was still recording how many were stamped on each day, and whether one must imagine the machine happy.

The Protagonist found himself overcome with a nostalgic longing for that terrible vending machine coffee. He retraced his steps back across the factory floor. Something felt different than it felt in his memory. When he walked this floor years ago, people looked at him. Even if no words were exchanged, eyes locked on one another, a half-smile and subtle nod of recognition passed between two souls. A silent message of "I acknowledge your existence." This time, the Protagonist went unnoticed and unacknowledged. He passed back through the room with the metal lockers and peeling beige paint into an adjacent breakroom. An array of brightly-colored plastic chairs sat motionless around wobbly tables, several of which had had their legs inelegantly balanced by wads of paper napkins. Overhead, a multitude of fluorescent bulbs bathed every corner with intense but noisome light. The vending machine still stood in the same place where the Protagonist had exchanged words with the pretty girl years ago. He pressed the buttons for coffee; black, two sugars. A paper cup fell down from some internal repository and into position. The machine whirred and vibrated for a few seconds, but poured no liquid into the cup. Then it fell silent and dead. Disappointed, the Protagonist took the empty paper cup for no other reason than to have something to hold while he inspected the room.

He opened the refrigerator. It was functioning, but there was no food inside except a single half-empty jar of mustard. The freezer compartment was empty as well, other than a strong, stale odor. He opened the cabinet doors that hung from the wall above the melamine countertops. The cabinet contained a cache of old coffee mugs; each one unique in shape and size and color, slathered with trite puns or logos for long-shuttered local businesses. Some bore the scars of repeated use– chips and hairline cracks. The insides of many of the mugs were stained with the brown, uncleanable residue of a million refills of coffee. And every mug in the entire set was slightly dusty, indicating they had not been used in a long time. Their owners were by now long ex-employees who had most likely forgotten that they ever once possessed them. In another cabinet were a box of party supplies; a roll of bunting, a paper sign that said "happy birthday," a box of garishly-colored, half-burned candles. In a drawer under the melamine counter was a pile of mismatched silverware, comingled with numerous plastic knives, forks, and crumpled napkins that had accompanied innumerable take-out orders. The Protagonist picked up a simple cake server and stared at it with wonder. How many times in the past was this used to serve people at retirements and awards celebrations and holiday parties? It didn't spontaneously appear here; it had a history. Someone, a secretary or whomever, had once purchased it on a company account and placed it in this drawer. For years it performed its function. But now those memories were lost to time. He wondered if it felt lonely sitting unused in the dark drawer? Was he the first person to touch it in months? Years? Decades? His mind wandered and he imagined a world after an apocalypse, when no one was left. The brick walls of this factory were strong and solid, they would undoubtedly stay standing for many, many years, even if empty and unattended. And for that time, this mundane object would lie in its drawer waiting patiently. Its handle shaped to comfortably fit a hand that would never again come, its blade designed to cut a cake that would never again be baked. Centuries from now, the factory would finally falter and fall to ruin, and the cake server would remain crumpled and crushed under a pile of bricks, slowly disintegrating, slowly losing its form and its status as an object independent from its surroundings, slowly awaiting the heat death of the universe.

A bell rang out in the distance. Immediately afterwards, the Protagonist heard a shuffling coming down the hallway, as if several people were approaching. He placed the utensil back in its drawer and sat down in one of the brightly-colored, plastic chairs. Several robots entered the room, some on legs, some on wheels. They queued up at the vending machine without acknowledging the Protagonist's presence. "No, after you," one said to its coworker, as it backed away with something akin to a bow.

"Thank you, you are very kind," replied the second robot. It pressed the buttons for coffee; black, two sugars, and waited patiently as the machine dispensed an empty paper cup. It took the cup and sat down. Other robots followed suit, until there were at least ten of them sitting around the wobbly tables in groups of twos and threes.

"Another day, another dollar, eh fellas?" exclaimed one robot, as it slumped in its chair. Inexplicably, it seemed truly tired.

"I'm looking forward to the weekend, that's for damned sure," said another. Several more mumbled their agreement.

"You guys get weekends off?" said the Protagonist, surprised. "How does that work?" The robots completely ignored him and the single conversation across multiple tables soon broke down into several competing ones amongst individual sub-groups. The Protagonist sat and listened quietly as the robots talked and talked. Mostly they talked about work. They talked about the pros and cons of the new schedule. They talked about whether they would get a smaller bonus than usual this year. They talked about how maintenance needed to restock the toilet paper more frequently. They talked and talked. The Protagonist tried interjecting himself into a conversation a few more times, but his comments went unacknowledged, and so he resigned himself to just listening in, as he had done at the neighborhood bar earlier that evening. It was still better than being alone.

In many ways, the conversations he overheard were the same as they had been when he worked there, but somehow subtly even more hollow. He learned that management was hoping to start thinking outside the box in the next quarter, but that they needed to have all their ducks in a row first. They wanted the departments to synergize more, but would have to run it up the flagpole for corporate approval first. So, they were going to have to take a step back and look at things from the 30,000-foot view before they pushed the envelope. Of course, the robots were tired of being asked to give 110% and having to reinvent the wheel every day. But, what were you going to do? At least it was a paycheck.

    The Protagonist had been much younger and more easily disillusioned when he worked at the factory some years ago. He remembered the conversations like this. He rarely, if ever, participated. Working together brought a connection of course, but a surface one, built on surface commonalities. Back then, the Protagonist sought deeper connection; discussions of art and philosophy and abstract political theories. But whenever he reached out on topics more profound than the fortunes of local sports teams or whether the coming rain was good for his lawn, his comments fell on deaf ears. "Are you some kinda Socrates?" one older coworker told him mockingly. The sting of that minor rejection still rang in his ears. The Protagonist had fallen mostly silent after that, being unsure of himself and insecure about how he was being perceived. His coworkers in those days took his silence for contempt, and felt little compulsion to invite him into their conversations. He took to bringing a book to read during breaks, solely so he wouldn't appear desperate for company.

"Any of you folks catch the game last night?" said one of the robots.

"I can't believe that call in the 3rd quarter. Them refs are blind, I tell you." It shook its head in disbelief.

A robot sitting at another table waved a claw in the air dismissively. "Can't blame it all on the refs. Our guys just didn't have their head in the game." A few others nodded in agreement, or disagreement. The Protagonist had never cared much about sports, or what brand of weed killer was best for his lawn, or how the traffic had been getting worse these last few years. He didn't care that gasoline was now ten cents more per gallon than before the last election, or which political party was more to blame for the increase. He never cared about the petty resentments co-workers had for one another, or the sycophantic jockeying they did to position themselves for their next promotion. It was tiresome and banal and pointless. But on this cold and lonely night, bonding over trivialities seemed preferable to the alternative.

He chimed in with a direct question about the game. But no one seemed to hear him. He got up from his seat and walked around the room. No one's head turned or followed his path. He came right up behind one of the robots and waved his hand in its face. It didn't react. Only then did the Protagonist notice that it didn't have eyes. It didn't have ears. None of them did. At least not eyes and ears recognizable to a human. They couldn't perceive him at all. If the robots could perceive each other, it must have been through some sort of radio wave, forever invisible and undetectable by the Protagonist.

One robot who had been sitting at a table near the refrigerator rose slowly, "man, my aching back," it said glumly. "Well, back to the grindstone." It tossed its unused paper cup into the wastebasket and moved towards the door. The other robots rose one by one and followed, continuing their insubstantial conversation about last night's game as they receded down the hall and out of earshot. The Protagonist was again left alone in the empty break room. There was a slight sound from inside one of the lower cupboards that might have been a mouse, or might have been nothing at all.

The Protagonist looked down at his empty paper cup and sighed. As he absentmindedly spun the cup, he noticed that it had some words printed on the side. It said, "Are you a winner?" Underneath the question were printed five playing cards that made up a poker hand; a pair of fours. Not much of a winner. Unwilling to be disparaged by a paper cup, he rummaged through the trash bin and pulled out all of the cups discarded by the robots. He piled them into groups on the wobbly plastic table. Each cup had a different hand. The best one he could find had a full house— aces over eights. He dumped the rest back in the trash, flattened the winning cup, and placed it carefully in his coat pocket, for luck.

Still forlorn, he exited the break room and wandered down a dimly lit hallway lined with darkened offices. For the most part they looked empty and unused. A few had no furniture at all, a few had desks and chairs and filing cabinets piled to the ceiling. Two or three showed some signs of having been occupied in the recent past, with binders and pencils and sticky notes and awards engraved onto clear lucite monoliths. The floors were covered in a tight weave of olive-brown carpet, its repeating pattern occasionally interrupted by dark and irregular stains. The overhead fluorescent lights were not on, but a glow came from the end of the hallway, partially illuminating everything in harsh shadows. Most of the doors he passed had had their nameplates scratched out or taped over, but a few were still legible even though the employees referenced by those names were doubtless long gone. He hesitated for a moment when he saw a name he thought he recognized. The Protagonist reached out and touched the grooves that made up the letters carved into the plastic sign.

Instantly, he remembered a day from years ago. He'd take a long weekend away, he couldn't remember the exact reason why, something about a summer sun. He returned to tears. The entire organization had been disrupted while he had been off-shift. Gossip was rampant about a middle manager who had been touring the production floor and had gotten too close to one of the stamping machines. Some piece of errant clothing must have become caught and he was pulled inside. In a split-second he was crushed beyond recognition.

There had been no time to even scream. "Thick blood and pulp was slowly running down the sides of the machine and pooling on the floor," he had been told. But by the time the Protagonist was back at work, all physical traces of the event had been scrubbed away. The emotional traces; however, remained for the rest of the Protagonist's employment. Coworkers who bore witness to the tragedy would regularly console each other in hushed voices, or cry together in bathroom stalls. They met at bars to erase the trauma of that day with alcohol. The Protagonist, having not directly seen the event, and not knowing the poor soul who'd died, had no strong emotional connection to it. He felt bad about his absence of sadness, but only because he felt left out of a shared experience that seemingly brought everyone else closer.

    The Protagonist peered into the deceased middle manager's darkened office and got the impression that it hadn't been touched since the incident. It wasn't being preserved as a shrine; it's just there were plenty of empty offices that could be used by whomever the employee's replacement had turned out to be, so no one had taken the time to empty this particular office. Documents lay strewn on the desk describing now long-completed projects, and charts and graphs were tacked to the wall, containing now out-of-date projections. A single pencil covered with teeth marks lay near a disconnected phone. A whiteboard still had some writing on it, although now smudged beyond recognition. The only indication that the employee wasn't coming back was a stack of unopened condolence cards which had been carefully placed in the deceased employee's inbox along with some other mail.

The Protagonist closed the office door as a sign of respect and continued down the hallway in the direction of the light, eventually arriving at the single inhabited office in this wing. Inside sat a solitary man behind a desk, eating a comically-large sandwich. He wore a short-sleeve, white dress shirt and a gaudy, polyester tie that hadn't been tied quite right. What was left of the man's hair valiantly, vainly, yet unsuccessfully attempted to obscure his impending baldness. Plastic three-ring binders littered the floor around the man's feet. The sandwich was dripping brownish sauce down his arm and onto whatever papers were directly in front of him. "Oh, hey." The man said, wiping his mouth with a paper napkin.

The Protagonist greeted him in response. "I used to work here."

"Did you?" He crumpled up the napkin and tossed it towards the trash can.

"I think I did, but that was long ago." The Protagonist peered at the man behind the desk closely. It was hard to see at first because the years had been less than kind, but he thought he recognized him as the coworker who would incorrectly record how many lids had been stamped in a notebook. "See you're still working here even after all this time."

"Well, I couldn't turn down the promotion. I mean, look at this office. Sweet, huh? Before this I only had a desk stuck in a corner of a hallway."

"Looks like you certainly made something of yourself. You've come a long way since you were walking the floor, recording how many lids had been stamped." He hoped his comments about the man's former duties might jog his former coworker's memory, but the man gave no indication it had. It would have been nice to have been remembered. "Things sure have changed around here, huh?"

"Well, that's progress I guess." He shrugged and took another bite of his sandwich. "Nothing ever stays the same. People come, people leave. Management keeps suggesting new ways to make things more efficient, more profitable. New technology and new products require reconfiguration of process lines. That kind of stuff." He waved his hands around at the binders that filled the room. "That's what all these reports are about." A piece of lettuce flew out of his sandwich and landed on the floor, limply.

"I saw some of the robot workers. I guess there aren't any people around anymore. I think I'd miss the sense of comradery. Did everyone get replaced for profits or for safety?"

"No idea. That sort of decision is above my level. I hear they're better at keeping the Erelim from pilfering gears out of the factory equipment. But, it was a necessity, because, you know, there aren't as many people around these days to answer the help wanted ads. And even if you do hire someone, a lot of people don't..." He hesitated for a second, "...don't stick around that long."

The Protagonist looked down at the floor, "yeah, I get it," he said. "But I feel bad for you. It has to be lonely being here all by yourself."

"Oh, I'm not the only one here, no no heavens no. There's another guy too, we're best buds."

"Nice guy?

"Well... can't say. He's here during the day shift and I work nights. We never actually cross paths; at least I don't think we have. Unless you are him?" He looked at the Protagonist with a melancholy hope in his eyes.

"I'm not."

"Are you sure?"

"Pretty sure."

"Darn, I was hoping to meet him someday. He has good penmanship. On the notes he leaves on my desk. Every day I come in and there's a letter on my desk with production updates. Every day, rain or shine." The man pointed to a binder on a shelf overstuffed with the letters. "I've saved every single one. I always write back at the end of my shift too. That's why I can't ever quit. If I left, he would be lonely. I'd never do that to him. Imagine if he came in one morning and there wasn't a note waiting for him from me?"

"What if *he* quits?" he said as the man passed him the cherished binder from off the shelf.

The man was taken aback. "He wouldn't do that. I mean, leave me all alone here? He couldn't. As I said, we're best buds. As there are less and less of us, we old-timers have to cling to each other more and more, don't we?

They say that this company isn't just a large faceless conglomerate, it's a family. Right? The smaller we get the more like a family we become. The coworkers that are still here, the real ones, they'd never just abandon me. That's not how family treats family."

The Protagonist perused through the binder that the manager was so proud of. It contained sterile notes about production quotas, to-do lists of minor maintenance that needed to be performed, and other bureaucratic trivialities. He noticed that the handwriting in the notes varied measurably over three distinct time periods throughout the binder. The Protagonist chose to keep that information to himself. "Looks like you and him are very close. Or you and her?" He handed the binder back. "Or you and it," he mumbled under his breath. "Maybe you'll meet at a Christmas party or someone's retirement."

"Fingers crossed."

"So, what is this factory making these days? What's the new product?"

"Can you keep a secret?"

"I don't have anyone to tell."

The man smiled devilishly. "Good, I mean, I really wanted to spill to someone about this, but honestly, except for my best buddy, I don't really have anyone to tell either. And he almost certainly already knows. So, I'm glad you came. Take a look at this." He opened a drawer and pulled out a single piece of wrapped candy, placing it gingerly on the desk in front of the Protagonist.

"Candy?"

"No. Well, yes, candy, but it's more than candy. This is something special."

"How so?"

Ok, so, who likes candy? Think about it. I mean, *really* likes candy?" He didn't wait for a response. "It's kids, right? Kids like candy."

"Adults like candy too."

"Yeah yeah, candy's delicious, but us adults, we can take it or leave it. It's not something we obsess over. But kids, they can't get enough, they'll eat it and eat it 'til they get a tummy ache. And you know why?" The Protagonist didn't have an answer. "This is what R&D figured out. It's because somehow candy tastes *different* to a child. It tastes better somehow. But it's not the sugar that changes, sugar is just sugar, right? So it must be our *brains* that change when we grow up. Works the other way too. Give some coffee or a glass of gin to a five-year old and they'll spit it out. Tastes gross. Something about how people experience stuff changes as they grow up. I don't know, it's all sciency mumbo-jumbo that's beyond me. But the important part is that this item in front of you isn't just 'candy,' the sugars are specially formulated to taste not like sugar tastes now, but exactly the way you remember it tasting back when you were a kid."

The Protagonist picked up the wrapped treat. "I guess I can see why that would sell."

"It's going to be huge! Imagine the marketing– 'Be able to experience something again for the first time, before you got all jaded and boring!' And so much healthier for you than an adult treat like a cigar or a belt of scotch." The wrapper was decorated with the cartoonish face of a small child bearing an impossibly huge grin.

"I guess so. But what about all those tummy aches?" he said jokingly.

"Well, there are still a few kinks to work out. Some minor side-effects. That's why it's just a prototype for now. Here, have some more. Just don't tell anyone." He placed a handful of sweets on the desk, which the Protagonist put in his coat pocket. The man changed the subject. "So, you really worked here once, huh? Why did you leave this place anyway? I can't imagine you found a better employer."

59

"I think it must have been just a temporary job, for the summer or something. It was never supposed to be a long-term gig. No, that doesn't sound true. Maybe I guess I didn't feel like I fit in. Everyone else seemed so into working here. Solidarity and all that. I guess I felt like an outsider, watching everyone else through a pane of glass. Maybe it was a self-fulfilling prophecy in the end. People expected me to leave, so they didn't get to know me which made me not feel welcome."

"Things are much different now of course," the man replied. "The current team members are all super well connected. By radio waves. I think they may even share a brain somewhere down in the storage room closet. Every time we have to bring a new robot in, it's just a few button presses and bam, it's like they've been part of the team forever."

"Since you bring it up, are there any openings now?" the Protagonist said hopefully, "I mean, for people?"

The man put down his sandwich and leaned back in his chair. "Well, this question is implacably hard and inevitably difficult to answer."

"I could maybe pick up a shift or two..."

"The interesting and critical response to this question is: no."

"On like weekends or nights..."

"I'm not sure you'd really fit in any more. You are a person, a human being, or so I assume. In this new regime, the workers are all silicon and epoxy energy enlightened by line current."

"But there's lots of empty offices, right in this very hallway. Surely no one would mind if..."

"I suppose you could leave a resume at the front desk if you must, but I have to warn you, we lost our secretary last year, so it's unlikely that anyone will ever see it lying there. At least until we hire a new secretary, but that's improbable since there is no one to collect and distribute the resumes we receive from secretarial applicants."

The Protagonist understood. He dropped the subject. It wouldn't have been the same as he'd pictured it in his mind anyway, even if he did return. Whatever the dynamic had been in the past, it would inevitably be different now. A door once closed remains forever closed. A now a palpable air of awkwardness hung over the conversation. "Ok, well, I should probably be going."

"Yeah, I'm behind on all these reports I have to fill out."

The Protagonist stood up. "Thanks for the candy, at least. It was good to catch up." The man returned to his sandwich without acknowledging the Protagonist's departure. The Protagonist hesitated for a second at the door, as if one more question was on his lips, but only for a second. He turned and walked down the hallway silently. As he receded, he heard the man talking and almost returned, but the man was just talking to his sandwich. "Mmm. Does steak love lettuce?" was the last intelligible thing the Protagonist heard him say.

3

It didn't appear to be raining, but the tiny ripples that vibrated and distorted the streetlights' reflections in the puddles scattered across the road suggested otherwise. The Protagonist had hope that his short sojourn in the factory would have warmed him, but somehow, as he walked the desolate streets again, he felt even colder than he did before. Maybe the wind was rising. He pushed the brim of his hat lower against his forehead and pressed on.

He soon came to a cinder block building that abutted the sidewalk. The face of the building was painted off-white and bore the cracks and stains of age. Towering above was a neon sign, slowly rotating on its pole. In earlier times, it had read "Threnody Liquors" but all the bulbs were burned out save for the N, O, and D. The street in front of the store was lit by bright overhead lights in a futile attempt to ward off any ne'er-do-well's intent on lurking in dark shadows at this late hour. As he approached, he spotted several hooded figures loitering by the entrance and around a corner that extended down an unlit, seemingly endless alley behind the store. The ominous figures leaned impiously against the wall in twos and threes, talking in low voices and sharing cigarettes or swigs from bottles. The Protagonist's body tensed with, if not exactly fear, perhaps anticipation and dread. He was alone and unguarded. His first thought was that they must be fugitives, or vagabonds, ready to pounce upon a lone traveler as he passed. However, as he grew closer, he saw that was untrue; they were nothing more than boys. They slouched in rough denim jackets and hoodies pulled tightly around their temples, arms crossed against their chests to protect themselves from the chill rain. Their words were deep and guttural and almost foreign to his ears, making references and expressing idioms he could never hope to understand at his advanced age. As miserable as the weather was, it was apparent that the teens were content to be here together on this dark and rainswept street. Occasional chuckles arose. Two kids playfully slapped each other on the back in solidarity over some unheard quip. One boy came out of the store with several sodas and candy bars to share. The Protagonist wondered what life circumstances existed for these young souls that made leaning against a cement wall in the middle of a rainy night preferable to being ensconced in a warm bed. But he had no answer to that, and so quickly put the question out of his mind.

As he passed, one young boy, who couldn't have been more than thirteen, said to him, "Hey, got a smoke?" without looking up. His companion shot him a worried glance and slapped him on his arm. The boy's eyes then locked on the Protagonist's. A panicked expression crossed the boy's face. "Oh, sorry Mister," he said sheepishly.

The Protagonist walked on. "Dumbass," he heard the boy's companion whisper in admonition. Looming above the store was an overpass that allowed the cars going north and south above from having to stop for the cars going east and west below. A tall fence had been erected on the overpass. It curved inward slightly to deter climbers. Someone had once hung a sign made of a bedsheet from the fence, but it had long since been blown to unreadable tatters. A few more boys stood on the overpass, keeping stoic watch over their brethren below. A car passed the Protagonist, splashing muddy water onto the sidewalk in front of him. As it sped by, the boys on the overpass drew eggs from their pockets and threw them down onto the car, resulting in several loud, wet thumps as they landed on its roof. The car flashed its brake lights for a second, but then continued driving. As the boys fled down the street and into the darkness, they gleefully cheered as if they had slain a dragon with their assault. The Protagonist continued eastward.

Even from several blocks away, he could tell that the street he was walking on would soon end, as ahead of him lay a zone of infinite blackness. It was the gateway to a park, the largest in the city. As he trudged on, the buildings fell away behind him and he was soon surrounded by trees and a darkness that was only dimly held at bay by an occasional lamp that beamed feeble, yellowish light from above the walking path. Even the noise of the city seemed to recede into quiet. The branches of the canopy were leafless and vibrated audibly, though invisibly, as the wind gusted through them. He reached an opening that led to the shore of a large pond. It was easy to imagine that, in warmer and brighter times, children would play here. A dock held a dozen paddle boats constructed in the shape of swans. The way they had been tied up for the winter made it seem as if they were desperately huddled together against the cold. Their dead, plastic eyes stared at the Protagonist as he passed.

It was as good a place as any for a rest. He sat down on a park bench that had been oriented to provide the best view of the lake, the boaters, and a small playground consisting of little more than a set of limply hanging swings. He appeared to be alone. Past the lake and the trees towered some of the tallest buildings in the city; buildings which had undoubtedly been constructed to provide their residents a magnificent view of the park below. The Protagonist imagined the view from that height. At this hour, the park must have seemed an impenetrable, blank darkness hollowed out from the otherwise illuminated city blocks.

Absentmindedly, he found himself counting windows. He lost count after at least fifty. "There must be several hundred different apartments in that one building alone," he thought to himself. Several hundred people whom he would never meet. Just in that one, single tower were several hundred homes filled with couches and beds and cake servers and memories and the smells of exotic meals, and the sounds of arguments and wails of tragedies and drawings hanging on the fridge that had been brought home from school by a child, and faded photographs of relatives long deceased. And he would never be an observer to any of it. He would never know those people.

    He then multiplied that thought by all the buildings he could see rising up around him. At least twenty more stood side-by-side right on that one block alone. Then multiplied again by all the other blocks in the city, and then multiplied again by all cities in the world. His imagination built a Venn diagram of experience. A small circle in the middle represented the furthest extent of his world. A few other circles intersected with his; some, like the woman from earlier tonight, only briefly touched him in one shared moment, others overlapped more significantly. But outside of his circle were millions, billions of other circles, existing in all directions, that never touched his circle at all.

Those experiences were forever unknowable to him. He felt small and insignificant and very lonely. The sky cleared of clouds, and the park brightened slightly in the moonlight. The Protagonist's eyes drifted upwards. Like they are in most cities, the heavens above were a dull, gunmetal gray, not pure black; but a few of the brightest and most persistent stars were visible. Beyond them lay millions of other stars, hidden from view, but there nonetheless. Further beyond were millions of galaxies– each filled with millions of stars of their own, each star surrounded by planets, each planet dotted with cities, each city filled with towering buildings filled with hundreds of apartments filled with beings the Protagonist would never know.

    Since he did not know them, or share their experiences, those people couldn't exist as discrete entities in the Protagonist's reality; they were each just a vague, smeared-out, superposition of all the probabilities that a person might potentially be. The Protagonist then came to the unpalatable conclusion that if that were the case, then logically, conversely, he must not exist in their realities either. Every observer experiences the world from a unique perspective, and so creates their own unique universe through their observation. Billions and billions overlapping universes, created by billions and billions of people out there, living full and complete lives, each in a unique universe that partially, but not completely, overlaps all the others. And in almost all of those universes, the Protagonist simply didn't exist. The only places he could truly say he existed were in the minds of those vanishingly few souls who remembered him, as well as in his own jumbled memories.

The overwhelming feeling of isolation was too much to bear, and he put his head in his hands and wept silently. After a time, he became distracted by a small beetle crawling past his foot. He followed the tiny thing as it went about its business. The bug stopped by his feet for a second, but only a second, and looked at him uncomprehendingly. "What a strenuous career it is that I've chosen! Travelling day in and day out," it said to him perfunctorily just before it crawled under a nearby trashcan. The Protagonist noticed several other beetles also wandering to and fro, a whole society of them scurrying around almost unnoticed in the dim light. "How about if I sleep a little bit longer and forget all this nonsense?" one insect bemoaned to its neighbor as they passed. A moth skittered through the air drunkenly. A worm thrashed about, fighting for its life in a tiny puddle. Undoubtedly, the underbrush in the park contained generations of rats and squirrels and moles nursing their young in makeshift burrows. An entire safari of creatures, playing out their stories in this one square acre, oblivious of the wider world around them.

A droplet of rainwater landed on the Protagonist's hand. He lifted it to his face and stared at it intently. Inside the droplet, barely visible, was a swirl of dust particles it had accumulated in its fall from the heavens. Beyond the dust lay countless single-celled organisms, happily living and eating and reproducing and dying inside the droplet, oblivious to the beetles and the worms and everything else existing in the park. The Protagonist strained to add all these tiny circles to his Venn diagram, but it quickly became too impossibly large to hold it all in his head. An infinity of infinities. So he just sat back up and let his mind go blank.

The Protagonist had almost fallen asleep when a man walked by, "What a strenuous career it is that I've chosen! Travelling day in and day out," he said perfunctorily as he passed. Before the Protagonist could formulate a response, the man had continued onward out of earshot, circumnavigating a path around the lake. The chains of the playground swings began creaking as a light breeze arose. He imagined children swinging back and forth. Had he ever been on a swing? He couldn't remember any specific instance of ever being on one, but it must have happened at some point. He considered getting up and sitting on the swing now, but then he remembered the candy in his pocket. He opened the wrapper that depicted the cartoonish face of a small child bearing an impossibly huge grin. Inside was a jelly-like blob. It was blue and dusted in white powder. In a trick of the dim light the candy appeared to almost glow in the dark. The Protagonist sniffed the treat cautiously. It had no smell. He pressed it gently against his tongue and experienced the unremarkable taste of sugar. It didn't seem poisonous. He put the entire candy in his mouth and began to chew.

He watched as the children ran back and forth. While they called out to each other with laughter and grinning faces and expressions of wonder and joy, they moved their small bodies in an entirely contradictory manner. Under the cover of a child's game, they circled about the playground like predators, looking for a moment of weakness to strike. They feinted and pushed at one another, trading tags and touches and slaps and trips. They fought for dominance. It was tribal, primal, feral. Groups forming and reforming around the strongest competitors. The smallest and weakest slowly but inexorably becoming outcasts– taunted and ridden-down by fiercer rivals. "Poindexter!" "Four-Eyes!" "Dork!" they shouted and hurled stones at anyone who did not possess the temerity to return fire. Innocent grins took on the appearance of the baring and gnashing of teeth. Soon, a child was down on the ground, skinned knee, face in the dirt. The other children, still bursting with laughter and with grinning faces and eyes wide with wonder pounced like lions upon the unfortunate one in a hail of fists and fury. It was over almost as soon as it began. Dominance determined through tears and screams of anguish and cries for mercy. The tribal order was settled. The victorious children once again played together harmoniously as they schemed internally over the choice for their next target. The losers cowered at the fringes, licking their wounds.

The Protagonist's mouth was filled with the taste of mud and blood. He spit the candy onto the ground in disgust. It bounced off the shoe of a person sitting on the bench next to him. The Protagonist spit once more to fully clear the unpleasant taste from his mouth. "You don't look so good," the person said. It was a man, in his middle-age. His eyes were partially hidden behind small, teacup glasses. His head was crowned with a mop of wiry blonde hair that appeared faded and washed-out. He was unshaven and unkempt and was clad in what appeared to be a stained, white lab coat. On his lap was a sheaf of papers at least two inches thick.

"I'm sorry, I didn't see you sit down," said the Protagonist. The strange man was uncomfortably close and smiling broadly. "Are you someone important to me?" he asked the man.

The strange man did not respond to the question but instead said, "Do you want to see what I have here?" He tapped the sheaf of papers. "I hate to bother you at this late hour, but I've just completed my life's work." He sighed. "And... well... I just really wanted to tell someone, you know? I'm very proud of it. But there aren't many people in the park at this hour. Please say you'll look at it."

"I suppose you can show it to me," replied the Protagonist. "But don't you have someone close to you that would be more interested than a random, unfamiliar person sitting alone on a park bench?"

The strange man became downcast. "I guess I've been too focused these last few years... on the work. I think I used to have friends. But if I did, I can't remember their names anymore. I had a brother once... but I'm pretty sure he died in the war. My colleagues have all rejected me as a kook. I... I don't have anyone." He paused for a second and attempted to sound more upbeat. "But it's worth it. My work... it's going to save us all."

"It would be nice to be saved. Go ahead, explain," he said sympathetically. The Protagonist thought to himself that listening to the strange man's story would at least take his mind off the vision of feral children.

The strange man grinned hopefully and he started turning the pages of his manuscript. "Did you know how scientists go about proving things these days...? They do it mathematically! It's true, you can prove everything with just abstract numbers. Some scientist simply writes equations on a piece of paper that say some phenomena like black holes or electrons or elementary forces or quantum fields and all the other bric-à-brac the universe contains *can* exist. And if something can exist then the equations hold that it *must* exist. And if it must exist then it does... it *does* exist. Everything in the universe exists because the math says it has to exist. You can't argue with math. Two plus two is four, that's just a fact."

The Protagonist looked down at the papers the strange man was pointing to. They were filled with scribbled equations containing not only recognizable numbers and letters, but also esoteric and unidentifiable symbols. "I've never tried to argue with math," he said. "But I'll take your word for it."

"So, here's the breakthrough," the strange man continued, "I've spent my life studying the universe and physics and math and equations and putting them all together in a million different ways to get to some fundamental truth about the nature of existence. At first, I couldn't connect it all into a single theory that would explain everything, so I kept studying and studying; field after field after field. Doctorate after doctorate after doctorate. The easy part of course was first devising a finite set of axioms that produced all possible true mathematical statements. But even after that, it took another decade of pouring over equations for it start to become clear. But here... if you look here on page eighty-six..." He pointed to a line of symbols on that page. "You see right here, you see what this means?"

"I see where you are pointing, but I don't understand what that means."

"It's clear as day!" he said animatedly. "This specific line proves... proves that God *can* exist. And if God can exist, God *must* exist. And if God must exist, then God *does* exist. It's right there in the physics. We don't have to take it on faith anymore! We have proof now. Hard, undeniable, incontrovertible proof. It's right here!"

"Ok." The Protagonist said skeptically.

"How can you not believe me...?"

"I want to believe you, I just don't know what most of these symbols mean." He pointed at one. "What is this one? It looks like a cartoon of an upside-down duck? And that one there looks like a ham sandwich?"

"Of course, I had to invent some new symbols for a few variables that had never been described before, but they are all defined in the extensive appendix..." The strange man flipped back and forth through his papers. "You can see here that this equation uses the curvilinear quantum field equation that I modified in the previous section but then applies an inverse Lorentz transformation into 6-D eigenspace...." He went on like that for several minutes, going back and forth through the manuscript, rambling in what was almost a foreign language. The Protagonist didn't understand a word of it. The strange man became disheartened. "Can't you... can't you see...?"

"I wish I could see. It would be a comforting thing to be sure of, certainly. But I'm afraid I'm not smart enough to understand the math. Unlike you, I haven't spent decades learning the fundamentals like you have. The way you describe how much work you've put in, I'm not sure anyone but you is going to understand the math. But if it makes you feel better, I'm willing to take it on faith that this is correct."

"But you are missing the point!" the strange man yelled. "The point is that this is *proof*, it's supposed to make it so you don't have to take it on faith. It's so clear to me; God, the machine elves, what happens after you cross the event horizon of a black hole, why there is evil in the world, what we are all supposed to be doing with our time here on earth. It's so clear right here in the equations... But I can't make you see... I dedicated my life to this..." He trailed off. The Protagonist felt sorry for the strange man. "If no one can understand, then it's just nonsense, isn't it? What's written on these pages, it's not transmittable... just asemic."

"Just because I don't understand it, doesn't mean it's nonsense. Maybe you could find some disciples and teach them what all this means, and they can go out and try to explain it to dummies like me..." He trailed off when it became clear that the strange man had stopped listening. The man stood up, spilling his treasured papers on the ground, and walked away, not saying another word. The Protagonist watched as the strange man followed the path circumnavigating the lake. He picked up the precious papers and brushed the dirt and water off of them. Maybe the man would come back for them, he thought. He had intended on leaving them on the bench, weighted down with a rock, but he found himself flipping through the pages. It was as comprehensive as it was incomprehensible. After paging through the work for a bit, the Protagonist stopped to ask one of the beetles scurrying past his feet if it understood what this guy was talking about. The beetle just shrugged and went on its way. It was too busy living its life to have time to worry about its place in the larger universe.

The final page ended with the words, "This final equation holds that I will try to explain this work to a man sitting alone on a bench in the park at night, but he will not understand a word. After that, all hope is lost." Next to the last sentence was an arrow pointing to a detailed drawing of a bedraggled man in a raincoat who was eerily similar to the Protagonist. He looked up, and saw the small figure of the strange man all the way on the other side of the lake. He was climbing up a tree with a rope in his hand. The Protagonist watched as the strange man tied the rope to a limb. "Wait, stop!" shouted the Protagonist, but the man was too far away to hear him. It would take too long to run around the entirety of the lake to arrive in time, so the Protagonist just stood impotently and watched as the strange man tied the other end of the rope around his neck and fell out of the tree, ending with a jerk and a wrench. The body slowly swayed in the light breeze. Soon after that, several Erelim, clad only in their eerie blue glow, appeared from the underbrush. The little things climbed over the man as he hung from the limb and began to go through the pockets of his lab coat.

The Protagonist again heard the creaking of the playground swings swaying. But this time he looked further afield and realized he had been mistaken. What he had thought was the sound of the swings swaying in the breeze was in fact the sound of other suicides swaying on the end of their ropes like strange fruit. The city of course had people on staff to take care of such things, but they only worked during the day, so by this time at night, the number of uncollected was starting to pile up. It gave the park an unpleasant character, and the Protagonist decided he didn't want to be there anymore. He pondered what do to with the document he still held in his hand. He considered just dropping it in a trash bin, but that seemed a bit disrespectful. He considered leaving it on the bench, in case someone curiouser and smarter than him wandered by. But the bench was already a bit damp, and it was likely to rain again before morning, so leaving it was functionally the same as throwing it away. In the end he rolled it up and stuffed it into one of the large pockets of his overcoat.

The Protagonist hurriedly left the park by the least disturbing route possible and soon found himself back on the streets of the great city.

4

The wide boulevard that ran parallel to the park was filled with sounds and lights, despite the late hour. A few restaurants were still open; waiters too timid to shoo the few lingering patrons back onto the streets. Through the windows one could view solitary souls dallying over the scraps on their plates, reluctant to complete their night out on the town and slink back to dark and desolate rooms in hopes of a few hours of troublesome sleep. The Protagonist trudged along at a steady pace, pausing briefly in front of an otherwise nondescript building that caught his interest. While it bore no sign or identification on its façade, each time the building's blackened doors opened, deep indigo and green flashes of light, as well as sidewalk-shaking sounds of industrial music, leaked out onto the sidewalk. A line of stylish people almost a block in length waited patiently for their chance inside the club. Angry young men, dapper in the latest fashion trends and with immaculately-coiffed hair, stood in groups near clusters of young women, scantily-clad in sparkly gowns, heavy makeup, and uncomfortable heels. No one in this queue was passé enough to hide their stylish clothes and fit young bodies within the confines of a jacket or heavy sweater. The girls shivered in the cold, damp air and tried to warm themselves with their breath and their hands. The Protagonist was chilled even under his overcoat and hat and felt a tinge of pity for their discomfort. "What are you looking at?" one girl shouted at him. "Pervert," shouted another. The Protagonist quickly resumed his walk. Half-hidden behind the line of party-goers, in an adjacent doorway, he could just make out the silhouette of a person lying face down on the floor, in tattered and mud-stained clothing, with a newspaper covering their head. Some unidentifiable fluid was leaking onto the sidewalk from underneath the body. The person did not appear to be breathing.

The lively commercial district the Protagonist traversed lasted only a few blocks, and consisted mostly of rows of now-closed storefronts shuttered with secure metal grates pulled down over big glass windows filled with bright signs announcing sales on exciting new products. Almost every light post and telephone pole was covered with ragged and faded posters still valiantly struggling to entice readers to come see a band or stage production that had occurred months ago. Soon, as the avenue began winding up a hill, the stores and restaurants gave way to a series of residential buildings. These appeared more modern than some of the antiquated architecture found in other parts of the city, albeit with little in the way of ornamentation or flourish to distinguish them from one another in any appreciable way. Some graffiti randomly peppered doorways and newspaper boxes, possibly added by nameless residents to tell their home apart from their neighbors. The scrawls were often in the form of inscrutable ciphers understandable only to their author. But, the Protagonist did read the words "No one is coming to save you" that someone had legibly scratched onto a plywood board covering a broken and abandoned doorway. The abandoned house offered him its black heart through open windows, but the Protagonist instead quickly hurried away.

At the very top of the low hill was a monument, encircled by a smattering of park benches that were in turn interspersed with some small patches of unkempt greenery. The monument consisted of a singular, granite obelisk that stood twice as high as the Protagonist himself. He approached it out of curiosity. Large brass letters that read, "TO OUR GLORIOUS DEAD," had once been hammered into the front side. However, several of the letters had long since fallen out and been lost, leaving behind only shallow, ghostly scars in the granite to mark their absence. The reverse side of the obelisk displayed several brass plaques, weathered a deep forest green with age, that acknowledged the heroic deeds of local citizens who had been killed in some now forgotten war. On the ground next to the plaques someone had lain a wreath consisting primarily of red cloth formed into the shape of poppies, bound to a wire backing. The wreath had fallen over, or been blown over, into a small puddle left from yesterday's rain. The cloth flowers were faded and stained with mud and soot from the passing cars. The Protagonist picked up the soggy memorial and leaned it against the monument in the most dignified manner he could. It dripped reddish liquid.

The Protagonist then sat on a bench opposite the memorial and contemplated. An occasional car passed by; its headlights causing the obelisk's shadow to rapidly sweep across the greenery like the hand of a clock. He considered the names etched on the memorial's plaque. Men, once made of living flesh and filled with dreams and hopes of the future, now reduced to nothing more than a list of half-illegible names on a tarnished stone in a park few people visited. And someday, like Ozymandias, even the stone would crumble into ruin and obscurity. The obelisk's shadow swept past him on several more circuits.

On the other hand, he thought to himself, war or not, was this not the eventual fate of us all? Whether blown to pieces on a battlefield defending a flag or quietly expiring in bed surrounded by weepy grandchildren, all flesh is inexorably reduced to such poverty. If that was a fundamental truth, it could be argued that any noble cause, even one that was not objective and eternal, presented as good of a reason to die as any other. In the absence of eternal and objective meaning, couldn't any temporary, subjective meaning suffice? "To give your life in service of something bigger than yourself," he thought, "at least I wouldn't have to die alone." The obelisk's shadow kept sweeping around past the Protagonist counter-clockwise with every passing car. "To be one with a multitude of others who've dedicated themselves to the same call to arms." He sunk deeper into the bench. The cars passed rhythmically one after another, engines purring. In the downtime between their passing, one could faintly hear the bass emanating from the club blocks away. He watched the shadows sweep by with narrowed eyes.

    A large explosion rattled the ground and woke him from his torpor. Some loose stones and mud spattered down from above, but he was still safe, protected by the sandbags and wood barricades piled up at the top of the trench. He instinctively reached for the rifle he religiously kept by his side. As the dust settled, he could see the sky above him, gray and clouded and teeming with barrage balloons. Puffs of black smoke occasionally drifted overhead, bringing with them the acrid scent of gunpowder and hot metal... and blood. A tricolored flag hung limp and dead from the top of a makeshift pole. He adjusted his helmet and his eyes started to come into focus. Soldiers from the Protagonist's regiment loitered in crouched positions all around him. Some were seemingly oblivious to the barrage raining from above, others cowered with a grimace of terror permanently etched on their faces. Two sergeants continued to nonchalantly play cards over a makeshift table. Propped up alongside them was the body of a lifeless private, open-mouthed with rigor mortis and staring blankly at the sky with dead, vacant eyes. The midsection of the private's uniform was stained black, and his feet were bare and unmuddied. Someone, presumably as a morbid joke, had placed a hand-painted wooden sign in the dead man's lap that read "Private Boots: R.I.P."

The Protagonist didn't recognize the dead man. "Was that his name... Boots?" he said.

"We never got his name," replied the first sergeant. "He wasn't here long enough."

"And can't read his name tag now. Fool got it all full of holes. Gonna have to give him a demerit for that," said the second sergeant.

"But the poor sap was kind enough to deliver me these new boots," said the first sergeant, "he even went to the trouble to break 'em in for me." The Protagonist noticed that the sergeant was wearing the dead man's shoes. The two gruff veterans laughed and went back to their cards. Another shell exploded somewhere overhead, raining pebbles and dirt onto the soldiers below.

There was naught to do until the shelling subsided or the regiment received new orders, so the Protagonist and the other men just sat and huddled and did their best to keep dry. Occasionally, messengers ran back and forth along the trench, ferrying unknown commands between faceless officers hidden away in unseen, underground bunkers. A light, greasy rain started to fall. A pair of orderlies passed by carrying a stretcher that held someone covered by a sheet. Only the wounded man's hand was visible as it dangled limply off the edge, nails filthy with black mud. The orderlies trudged along at a slow and methodical pace, implying that they held no hope that the man on the stretcher could be saved. A corporal rocked back and forth with closed eyes, tightly clutching a rosary and murmuring something that was only audible to himself and his god. Low conversations could be heard in the distance. From his vantage point in the trench, the Protagonist could glimpse shells flying overhead in both directions. Considering the extensive range of modern cannons, not to mention the fog and smoke obscuring the battlefield, he assumed that there was no possibility that the artillerymen firing the shells could see their intended target, or if they were true to their mark. They may not have had a specific target at all. They followed orders, loaded round after round, pulled the firing lanyard, and watched as the shells flew off into the clouds. An artilleryman in this nightmare would surely have to assume that they killed an enemy soldier, at least sporadically, but they'd never know with certainty. They'd never know if their actions helped turn the tide of the battle or were completely ineffectual. They'd never know whose death they caused, or anything about their victim; left with nothing more than the assumption, or the hope, that those torn apart by the shrapnel were, to some degree, less than human.

The Protagonist scrambled for a safer position between two piles of soiled sandbags left over from some now-forgotten construction. He found himself back-to-back with a young private who'd sought refuge in the same place. The private barely noticed the Protagonist's presence at first; he was preoccupied with something in his hands. It was a photograph. "Look at her," the private said to him, "isn't she a real basket of oranges? And a real hell-cat too, let me tell you."

The Protagonist agreed that she was very winsome. "She waiting for you back home?" he asked.

"Sure is. The day I shipped out, she told me she'd be true 'til the end of time. We're gonna get married as soon as this war is over. I write her every day."

"Does she ever write back?"

"I'm sure she does. She promised she'd write every day. It's just... It's hard for letters to get delivered here, you know? But I bet that when I rotate back to headquarters there'll be a whole pile of letters waiting for me, scented with fancy perfume." Something in the tenor of his voice implied that he wasn't sure of the truth of his assertion.

The Protagonist felt it was appropriate to be encouraging. "I bet there'll be some cookies and another photograph too," he said. The private smiled sadly. "With a great girl like that back home, what made you enlist and come all the way out to this blasted hellscape?"

The private looked at him quixotically. "What other choice did we have? This is important. If we don't hold the line here, they'll press on and invade our homes. I thought about what those brutes would do if they ever got their grubby hands on...." The private hesitated. "I mean, we can't just throw up a white flag and let those devils over there just take whatever they want, right?"

"No. I suppose we can't," replied the Protagonist. They sat without talking for some time after that.

"Hey buddy, do you got a girl waiting for you back home?" asked the private.

"I'm not sure. For some reason, I can't remember clearly right now," said the Protagonist. "Maybe I'm just bit shell-shocked."

"I know why I'm here. If you're not protecting someone special back home, what are you doing here?"

Just then, a large shell exploded somewhere very close by and caused a part of the earthen barricade to subside and collapse. While no one was injured, a pair of newly-inducted fusiliers that had been cowering and shivering under a corrugated tin sheet found themselves half-buried under the trench wall. The men were completely soaked in cold, dark mud, errant tree roots, and small stones. As they dug themselves out of the mess, one of the card-playing sergeants shouted towards them, "Watch what you're doing with my new boots. I don't want 'em if they're all dirty." The other sergeant chuckled ghoulishly. The two fusiliers looked blankly at each other. They were now completely black from head to toe, like reverse ghosts, with only their wide, white eyes standing out against the dark, wet mud that covered them completely. The Protagonist watched as those white eyes grew and grew with panic. One of the fusiliers made a break for it. Before anyone could stop him, he scrambled up the partially collapsed trench wall, over the top, and ran at full speed away from the enemy and towards the imagined safety of the rear. A short volley of machine-gun fire came soon after, but no one in the trench could see if the fleeing soldier made it or was mercilessly cut down. The Protagonist liked to imagine that he made it. The sergeants just shook their heads and went back to their cards. "Dumbass," one murmured to the other.

The second fusilier wandered off down the trench, shell-shocked and shivering, futilely hoping to find something dry with which to clean his face. The Protagonist followed. "Hey, hey... It's going to be ok." He said to the man. "Let me help you." He gently wiped the man's face with the sleeve of his uniform.

"I shouldn't even be here!" the man cried out. Pushing the Protagonist away, he kicked at a half-rotted post in anger and frustration.

"You can make it through. Me, you the rest of the regiment, we are all in this together."

"Speak for yourself," the man said dismissively. "I'm only here because father forced me to enlist. Said it would 'build character'. But he assured me he'd keep me far away from the real fighting. Just close enough to be able to brag to the lads at the club. How did I end up in this filthy hole with the rabble?" he shouted to the sky.

"Not letting those brutes and devils take whatever they want from us?" the Protagonist suggested.

The fusilier did not respond, other than to spit on the ground. "I would stab father in the face right now for a hot bath," he said dismissively and wandered off. The Protagonist sighed and returned to his position between the sandbags. The private who had been clutching the photograph was nowhere to be found, and the Protagonist was again left to his own thoughts. Sullen and grim-faced soldiers continually lumbered back and forth through the trench, moving like zombies. None acknowledged the Protagonist's presence. In hopes of establishing a solidarity of joint suffering, he endeavored to make eye-contact with each man as they passed, but their eyes were all dead and vacant.

He noticed that a reckless rifleman had imprudently stuck his head over the top of the sandbags to catch a glimpse of the enemy. The Protagonist rushed to him and dragged him back to safety. "Get down! What are you doing?!?" he shouted.

"Oh, don't worry about me," said the rifleman. I can't die."

"You're mad."

The rifleman shook his head. "No, not mad. I'm just immortal. Well, quantum immortal anyway. We all are. It becomes pretty obvious if you think about it. Have you been keeping up on the latest science? I've been reading it in the papers. The new theory from the lads in Copenhagen, they call it 'quantum superposition,' you know what that is?"

"I have no idea."

"It says that if there are two possible outcomes to an event, both are simultaneously true until you look at it. It's like coin flying through the air. It's not heads or tails until it lands and you look. While it's in the air it's both and neither at the same time."

"How does that nonsense stop you from getting your head shot off?"

The rifleman thought for a second. "Ok, let me try this another way. Close your eyes and imagine that you are dead. What is it like?" The Protagonist closed his eyes and imagined himself lying in a casket in a church. Mourners came and went as colored lights beamed down through stained glass windows. "You are imagining seeing yourself in a casket, right?"

"Yes, said the Protagonist. "It's a bit relaxing actually."

"But see, that vision is wrong. If you are dead, I mean actually totally dead, you can't be there to observe yourself lying there in a casket. A soul has no mechanism to observe itself not existing. It's impossible. That's quantum immortality. Say for example, I ran through no-man's land right now– there'd be a chance I'd get killed, and a chance I'd live. But we don't know which result will happen just yet. It's like the coin spinning in the air. We only know whether I lived or died once we observe the result, once we look at the coin lying on the ground. But if I'm dead, I can't observe the coin. And if I can't observe it, then quantum physics holds that specific result can't happen. And if I can't possibly be dead, then I must be alive. So

97

there you go, according to the latest science, I can never die."

"That's pretty optimistic. Putting your faith in crackpot theories like that," replied the Protagonist. "What if there were an afterlife? Some other dimension where you could look down on yourself being dead?"

"I don't think that science postulates an afterlife, but, hypothetically, if there were a place where you could... you could experience yourself not existing...? I guess that would be hell." The rifleman seemed quite convinced of his conjecture, and the Protagonist thought it best to not argue further, lest he accidentally disrupt the man's faith. Regardless of the ultimate truth of the rifleman's logic, it seemed to give him comfort, which is something everyone in the regiment, including the Protagonist, was in dire need of.

Due to the gray, overcast sky and the clouds of gunpower smoke drifting by, no one in the trench could see the location of the sun. It was impossible to tell how fast or slow time was passing while they waited for orders. However, at some indeterminate time after the Protagonist had discussed quantum superposition with the crazed rifleman, his probability wave collapsed when a pair of officers followed by a platoon of soldiers marched down the trench. They said nothing, but paused momentarily to allow the Captain to blow a whistle. They then resumed their march. The sergeants got up from their game of cards. "Ok, boys, you heard the signal. We're going over in five minutes. Suit up." Immediately, it almost seemed as if the very walls of the trench came to life, as muddy and filthy soldiers began to stir and emerge from every shadow. They straightened their uniforms as best they could, checked their weapons and ammunition, and lined up in their positions. Ladders were raised against the towering barricades, and the two sergeants took up positions at the head of the columns. "Masks," one of them shouted. The men all donned their gas masks. The Protagonist looked around at his compatriots through his rapidly fogging lenses. The soldiers now seemed otherworldly and demonic; a horde of faceless and fleshless wraiths made wholly of rubber, glass, and metal; bodies dripping with dark, wet filth and bristling with armaments. The sergeant peered timorously over the trench wall, waiting for the signal. "Affix bayonets!" All went quiet for seconds, minutes, hours, lifetimes. A large white balloon rose serenely overhead and floated over the trench.

Straightaway, the cannon barrage began, loud and fast and hard. The earth rumbled beneath the men's feet. "Forward!" exclaimed the sergeant.

The regiment poured forth into no man's land. From his position in the center of the horde, the Protagonist witnessed wave after wave of young men climb the ladders and rush headlong into the enemy. Machine gun fire echoed from every direction. When it was his turn, the Protagonist was pressed forward by the crush of men behind him and had no choice but to climb the ladder. The world between the enemy trench and his own was a scarred, colorless hellscape of mud and fog and barbed wire and bodies. Smoke and souls could be seen rising into the sky all around him. To his left and his right his compatriots were anonymous and unidentifiable in their identical uniforms. He saw many soldiers blown to pieces or cut down by gunfire before his goggles became too fogged to see anything beyond his own feet. "Forward to Glory!" he heard someone shout. He followed the sound of the voice and went forward. His blurred perception seemed to have transformed the men around him. There were riflemen and grenadiers, but now also shining knights in gleaming armor and winged hussars charging on horseback. Armored tanks squared off against war elephants bristling with archers clad in white linen. Chariots galloped through the broken ground in an attempt to flank a whole phalanx of pikemen. Swarms of spider-like drones levelled an entire detachment of helpless cataphracts with barrages of lasers and rail guns. Above the chaos, biplanes and jet fighters and zeppelins and nuclear bombers circled. In the confusion, the Protagonist lost sight of his unit, but he pressed on. He looked for familiar faces to guide him, but he was surrounded now only by beasts and monsters, screaming and howling for blood.

    The Protagonist stumbled through the broken wasteland until he tripped over something nauseatingly soft and squishy and tumbled headfirst into a deep shell hole, half-full of fetid water and rusted metal. As he righted himself, his boots sank knee-deep into thick mud, binding him in place. His rifle had fallen from his hands and was now lost. He pulled at the walls around him, but the loose, wet soil just gave way as he clawed at it. Above him, he could catch glimpses of shadows of soldiers running past, obscured by smoke yet illuminated in every flash of cannon fire. In the fog of war, no one noticed him trapped beneath their feet in this muddy ditch. A deafening roar of discharging weapons was the only thing he could hear, with any lulls in gunfire being filled with war cries and screams of agony. He tried to catch his breath, but that was not possible within the confines of his ghoulish rubber mask.

It was impossible to judge how long the battle raged on, but after a time, the fighting subsided. Artillery fell mostly silent; gunfire became sporadic. Only the whimpers of the wounded remained. The Protagonist wondered if his side had won or lost. There had been no cries of victory, but also no calls to retreat. He thought about the men of his regiment and where they might be. Some were certainly dead, others undoubtedly had made it to safety, but, if the mad rifleman was to be believed, for now they all existed as Schrödinger's cats, simultaneously alive and dead, until their bodies could be retrieved and accounted for.

He threw off his mask in an attempt to regain his humanity. Fumes of gunpowder and burning flesh immediately filled his nostrils. Without the myopic goggles obscuring his vision, the first thing he noticed was that the skyline above him was oddly beautiful now that it was on fire. From his position stuck in the mud, he couldn't see much of the battlefield, but if he contorted his body, he could peer over the crater's brim just enough to see a tricolor flag hanging dead at the top of its pole above the enemy position. The Protagonist squinted, but, due to the fog, or the smoke, or some strange trick of the light, he couldn't make out the flag's colors. He lowered himself back into the trench in despair. Bullets continued to zip by overhead intermittently, like flying insects, as those still alive in the trenches opportunistically fired in the direction of any suggestion of movement in the no man's land. He allowed himself to sink further into the mud. Perhaps, once night fell and the rain stopped, he could safely crawl back to his trench unseen.

Above him, somewhere out of view, he could make out the sound of labored wheezing. A fellow soldier, wounded and splayed out on the battlefield struggled to breathe, lungs slowly but inescapably filling with blood. The Protagonist could do naught but listen. He couldn't get free of the mud if he tried, and if by some herculean effort he were somehow able to lift himself up, he would most certainly be cut down by enemy fire well before he could render aid. He told himself that it was likely the man was beyond saving anyway. The sun struggled impotently to shine through a thick fog that descended across the battlefield, yet it provided no warmth to counteract the chill of the mud. The Protagonist shivered and wondered how long until nightfall. In the distance, cannons continued to fire indiscriminately.

The wounded man above him deprived the Protagonist of his solitude by stubbornly continuing to breathe. A delirium had set in, and he began to cry out. He cried out for help. He cried out for his girl. He cried out for his mother. The voice, though labored and muffled, was familiar. It was the private the Protagonist had spoken to earlier in the day; the one who'd shown him a photograph of his fiancé back home. If she had sent all those letters he'd claimed she'd sent, he would never get to read them. The Protagonist wished he could help the private, or at least be there to comfort him in his final moments. He considered calling out to him, telling him he was not alone, that he was loved. He considered offering to convey a final message to the man's fiancé. He closed his eyes and imagined a warm and sunny day after the war ended. He was walking up to a modest country house with a yellow ribbon tied around a tree in the front yard. He'd knock on the door and deliver the private's dying words and a blood-stained photograph to a weeping woman.

They would exchange a deep bond over their shared trauma. He'd lie and tell her that the private was brave and steadfast until the end.

However, the Protagonist stayed silent in his crater. He did not reveal himself to the wounded private. He simply listened in silence as the man's breathing became more forced and his struggled cries became quieter. Seconds, minutes, hours, lifetimes went by before the private finally went still. He died alone and scared. The sky did not betray the hidden location of the sun behind the clouds and smoke. The Protagonist shivered and wondered how much longer until nightfall.

He was suddenly roused from his slumber on the memorial bench by a car loudly backfiring as it drove past. He opened his eyes in time to witness the shadow of the obelisk sweep across his face clockwise. He sat up straight and rubbed the sleep from his eyes. He stood up and straightened his rumpled overcoat with his hands as best he could. Before he continued on his journey, he ran his fingers across the brass plaque of the memorial to see if he could find some mention of the private he'd dreamed of, but he realized he'd never bothered to learn any of his compatriots' names.

5

The Protagonist careened down the streets and alleys of the city, sinking further and further into despair. As he stumbled through dark, serpentine corridors, he passed innumerable faceless men, clad in drab, indistinguishable raincoats with turned-up collars and wide-brimmed hats, hurrying along on unknowable missions. The Protagonist's dream had left him feeling desolate and helpless. At every intersection, he turned again and again in an attempt to find room to be alone with his thoughts, but after each turn, he was confronted by further meandering sidewalks packed with more faceless men trudging past him without recognition or acknowledgment. Their constant presence only increased his sense of isolation. Above the street, darkened, unfriendly windows surrounded him, and the billboards were all leering. The world grew narrow and unfamiliar, as if a fog had settled in. Soon he was lost in the maze of twisted and misshapen streets that comprised the oldest part of the great city.

    The crisp sound of a church bell rang out from an unseen tower. Flakes of snow became visible as they descended in the beams of the streetlights. The Protagonist followed the sound of the bell, walking in the gutter to avoid the crush of pedestrians rushing along on the sidewalk. The pavement was soon dusted with a thin layer of white slush that soaked and stained his shoes. The bell rang out again, then a third time, seemingly closer with each peal. Since the Protagonist did not know his current location, he couldn't say if he was approaching the bell-tower or if the bell-tower was approaching him, but he began to feel that their trajectories were destined to intersect. He pushed his hat forward to shield his eyes from the falling snow, which left the nape of his neck vulnerable to the icy stings of snowflakes. With his vision obscured, he could no longer see the path ahead of him clearly, but he pressed forward staring at his own feet, trusting passersby to notice him and step out of the way.

Suddenly, the street noise surrounding him died down, as if a radio playing only static had been unplugged. It was a silent as the grave. He stopped and looked up. He was in the middle of a now-deserted block, standing in front of a gothic-styled cathedral. The faceless men in their drab raincoats had all disappeared from the streets. No cars passed by. Even the snow had stopped falling. From just above him, the church bell rang out one final time. He was here.

The building was ancient. The stones that made up the cathedral's edifice were blackened with soot from decades of exposure to the bustling city. Small drifts of white snow had nestled into the crevices, slowing melting and dripping water down the walls and buttresses. At the top of a short set of steps were two, thick wooden doors, propped slightly open despite the weather. A flickering of lights from inside drizzled into the street. The stones above the doors had been carved the with name "Cathedral of Saint Ovidius" by some stone carver no doubt long dead. Affixed to one door was a vinyl sign that flapped in the wind like a beckoning arm. It read, "Midnight Mass, All Are Welcome." The

Protagonist felt a sudden desire to be somewhere where all are welcomed, so he climbed the steps and entered the church.

The small foyer directly beyond the thick wooden doors held nothing but a display of pamphlets, some children's drawings of misshapen angels rendered in blue crayon, and a box soliciting donations for renovations. A cork board hung above the box, entirely empty save for several pushpins and a small banner that read, "Community Announcements." The floor here was mostly scuffed linoleum, but in a few places it had worn through sufficiently to expose the ancient hardwood floor that lay underneath. A non-descript door in the foyer was closed with a paper sign reading, "No Admittance" tacked to it with a pushpin. The Protagonist tried the knob anyway, but it was locked. Directly across from that door was an open archway, and the Protagonist stepped through.

As he entered the nave, he reached toward the font, but the basin was dry and empty. A few parishioners sat in the pews, mostly alone, but sometimes in groups of two or three. Some stared straight ahead blankly, others had their faces buried in prayer books. One elderly woman was rocking back and forth ferociously. No one was speaking. Against the wall was a table on which had been placed a large number of burning candles. The Protagonist picked up a fresh candle and moved to light it, but couldn't think of a single person he knew well enough to say a prayer for. He stood awkwardly for a time, and then sheepishly put the candle back down and sat himself in one of the pews.

"Terrible weather tonight, isn't it?" he greeted the person sitting closest to him in a hushed tone. The parishioner made no acknowledgment and gave no response, instead remaining focused on his reading. The Protagonist then turned around and caught the eye of a young woman sitting a few rows behind him. He waved and said hello, a little louder this time. The young woman responded only by tapping the side of her head, which the Protagonist inferred to be a signal that she could not hear him clearly. He turned back around, feeling slightly dejected. As he scanned the rest of the room, it seemed that the parishioners each existed in their own independent bubble, electing to spend their evening interacting with the divine, as opposed to interacting with the other mortals who had joined them for the service.

He became impatient with the silence and, out of boredom, reached for the hymnal stored in a pocket of the pew in front of him. When he pulled out the book, several pamphlets fell to the ground. One advertised a support group for alcoholics. It featured a photograph of a crowd of smiling people of all ages and ethnicities, toasting each other with cups of steaming black tea. They looked very happy in their shared sobriety. A second advertised a meeting for those who had experienced a recent tragedy to commiserate over their shared grief. It featured a photograph of a crying woman being hugged by another person and had the words "You are not alone" written at the top. A third pamphlet advertised a cooking class for diabetics. It featured a photograph of a festive table filled with innumerable healthy delicacies prepared for a large holiday gathering. The Protagonist mused that it was unfortunate he suffered no malady or misfortune sufficient to make him eligible to attend the groups.

The silence was broken by the sound of a door opening on the chancel. An enrobed priest entered. As he walked slowly and wordlessly to the pulpit, the heads of the parishioners turned, one by one, to face him. The priest quietly laid some papers on the lectern and spread them out.

The Protagonist was hopeful that he would receive some words of comfort from whatever sermon the priest had planned, or at least be distracted by some new idea or thought to help shake the terrible dream of war that was still at the forefront of his mind.

The priest's words gave no comfort though, as the sermon was not in a language the Protagonist understood. It was an old language, guttural yet lyrical in tone, but wholly unfamiliar to the Protagonist's ears. It wasn't Latin or Greek, he was sure of that, but something else, Coptic perhaps? Whatever it was, the faithful were rapt with attention. Every face stared directly at the priest as he delivered the liturgy. Since the words meant nothing to the Protagonist's ears, he soon became disinterested, but he could see that every other person in attendance was utterly mesmerized by the priest's performance. Several wept openly. Whatever comfort the Protagonist had vainly hoped to receive, the other parishioners were clearly receiving it. Oddly, they remained silent. There wasn't a 'hallelujah' or an 'amen' from a single person in the pews.

The priest spoke at length, pausing now and again to turn the pages of the notes in front of him. Through most of the sermon, his tone was flat and emotionless, but as he progressed, he began to speak louder and with a rising crescendo of passion. When he finally reached his conclusion, he raised his arms up in the air. At this signal, the faithful all stood and raised their arms in unison. Out of courtesy, the Protagonist similarly stood and raised his arms, although he did not know what he was standing for. Then, as suddenly as it began, it was over. Everyone lowered their hands and sat back down. The priest wordlessly picked up his notes and left through the same door from which he came. The clatter of his heels on the marble was the only sound. After the chancel door closed, the parishioners stood up and began milling about quietly. They placed their hymnals back in their pews. The young woman the Protagonist had attempted to speak to earlier walked to the front of the church and knelt directly before the dais to say a personal prayer. The Protagonist remained at a respectful distance, but after she had finished, he walked up to her and again said, "terrible weather tonight, isn't it?" but she passed him without acknowledgment. It was then that he noticed that the young woman had no ears. She was completely deaf. The Protagonist looked closely at the other parishioners and noticed the same thing. No one was speaking, but a few made gestures with their arms that could have been a form of sign language.

The parishioners silently exited, one by one, through a door at the back of the church, that led to an adjacent dining hall. The Protagonist followed. The hall was mostly bare and unadorned. One of the overhead fluorescent lights buzzed incessantly. A disused piano half-covered in a tarp had been pushed off to one side. A pile of filthy children's toys had been heaped haphazardly in a corner next to an empty bookcase and a stained and threadbare couch. Some folding tables and chairs leaned against one wall. In the middle of the room, a giant table, covered by several paper tablecloths, had been set with all sorts of food. Mismatched trays and bowls contained overly-cooked vegetables and casseroles and misshapen loaves of homemade bread. Several earnestly-decorated but lopsided cakes waited patiently to be consumed. The centerpiece of the table was a glistening ham the size of a large baby. The parishioners gathered and sat and ate and spoke to each other with their hands. The Protagonist stood aloof, off to the side, observing, but not participating. He wondered what they spoke of. Was it the quality of the meal? Was it the general comings and goings of their daily lives? Was it the sermon that they had just experienced? Without a common language, he had no way of knowing. They ate roughly; ripping and tearing the meats and bread with their bare hands. As they dined and socialized, no one approached the Protagonist, or invited him to sit, but they also didn't actively glare at him or do anything to make him feel uncomfortable. For a few moments, the Protagonist considered joining the table, but he was too intimidated to intrude on a large group of strangers. Besides, he told himself, he did not have much of an appetite. In the end, he took only a small crust of bread, and he only did so as to assure himself that he was actually physically present and not a just some sort of incorporeal ghost. The bread was warm and fresh, but tasteless in his mouth.

After lingering for a few minutes, he poured himself a cup of coffee from a large urn and left. No one was looking directly at him to see him wave on his way out. The heat of the beverage burned his fingers through the thin paper cup. He left the church through the foyer and the thick wooden doors that led back onto the street. The pavement had dried and the sky was clear and full of stars, although an icy chill remained in the air. The Protagonist sat on the steps to drink his coffee and ponder his next destination.

"Weather's improving tonight, isn't it?" said a voice from behind him. The Protagonist turned to see the priest walking out into the frigid night air. "I thought it was going to rain all night, didn't you?" he continued. The priest had changed out of his formal raiment into a comfortable gray tracksuit covered by a threadbare, woolen coat and a long, knitted scarf. As he approached, he unscrewed the cap on a metal flask. He sat down on the steps beside the Protagonist and took a swig. A city bus without a single passenger drove past, kicking up some leaves that had fallen into the gutter. "We don't get many walk-ins," the priest said, "especially for the late service."

"I guess I was feeling a bit lost... and cold," replied the Protagonist. "I wouldn't have intruded if I'd realize you catered to such specialized clientele."

"All are welcome. Of course, most folks are inclined to socialize with their own tribe, and people like you are far and few."

"People like me?"

"Those without a tribe." He handed the Protagonist the flask. The liquid inside was cheap rotgut, and it burned his tongue as it went down.

"Am I that obvious?"

"In my line of work, you can spot the signs of someone who's been abandoned." The priest took another draught from the flask. "Can I ask if you got any comfort being here tonight?"

"Not really. But I've grown used to that." They sat silent for a while, trading the flask back and forth. "Can I ask you a question?" said the Protagonist, "I was wondering what language you were speaking, when you were giving the sermon."

"Oh that," laughed the priest. "It's the policy of our diocese that all sermons must be in something called Adamic. It's a very old language. In fact, it's the oldest language. Every other language, every single language from all around the world can ultimately trace its lineage back to the primordial Adamic. They say it dates from before our ancestors first stood on two legs and migrated out of Africa, from before God cast down the Tower of Babel, back to a time when all of mankind spoke the same tongue. If you believe certain apocryphal scriptures, it goes back even further than that and was the celestial tongue of the Gods themselves before humans ever walked the earth. The idea for using it in our sermons is that it's more accurate because it's the only language unadulterated by mankind's bias."

"Was it hard to learn?" asked the Protagonist.

"I'd imagine so. Of course, I don't know a single person who can actually speak it. I sure don't."

"How do you give a sermon in a language you don't speak?"

"Not as hard as you'd think actually. Every week, a packet comes to me by mail from headquarters. It's got an entire sermon written for me, word for word. I haven't the foggiest notion what it means; they don't bother including a translation. But oddly, there's a lot of pronunciation notes included, so I just read it phonetically. I've been told that it is critically important to get the pronunciation exactly right. Sometimes the archbishop will send an evaluator to sit in the back and critique my oration. That's who I assumed you were at first."

"Seems like an odd aesthetic choice," replied the Protagonist. "I mean, if you don't know what you are saying, and the people listening don't know what they are being told, how can you be providing them with hope and comfort?"

"I've come to learn that when people crave hope and comfort, it's never about what specific words or facts someone tells them, it's about the emotions that stir inside of them when they hear it. None of my flock understand the language, sure, but none of them can hear a word of any language anyway. And yet that doesn't seem to matter. They come every week. Let me ask you a question; do you happen to know how they tune an orchestra?" the priest asked.

"Not really," replied the Protagonist.

"The musicians all take their seats, and then the oboe plays a long, unbroken A note. Every instrument in the orchestra has an A, so the musicians all match their note to the oboe's. That way everyone is tuned the same. It doesn't really matter if the oboe itself is a bit out of tune. As long as everybody is a bit out of tune the same way, the aggregate melody sounds good. That's me. I'm the oboe. People come here to tune themselves to my A note."

"I think I must be tone deaf then," joked the Protagonist. "I never feel like I'm in tune with anyone else's melody."

"The hardest problem in the world to cure is loneliness. It's the only problem a person can have where they can't turn to others for comfort," said the priest.

They continued to trade the flask back and forth for a few minutes. After a while, the Protagonist said, "can I confess something? It's not just other people I can't seem to connect with. I don't ever feel a connection to the divine. I never have. Maybe it's just too abstract for me to perceive. But, I close my eyes and there's... nothing. I say a prayer and it floats out into a void. Not even an echo comes back. It's like talking into a phone that's been disconnected."

"Honestly, I suspect that maybe everyone feels that way most of the time, on the inside at least," responded the priest. "That's why my flock pays to have someone like me point the divine out to them in an imperious stone building filled with overbearing symbolism. And even with my help, most people are lucky if they just catch a glimpse of it for a few fleeting moments before it's gone again. I suspect that those few who claim to regularly feel that connection are lying to themselves... or just insane. Happy and content maybe, but insane. Or on drugs. Different folks different strokes, whatever works for you. Who am I to judge?"

He took a deep swig and finished off what was left in the flask. "Ahh, what do I know, I just work here." The Protagonist didn't respond, but wondered if that was a confession that the priest was just as lost and alone as he was. He took a sip of the coffee he had poured himself earlier, but it had turned cold in the night air, and was acrid and bitter. He spilled it out onto the stone. Brown rivulets cascaded down the steps like a tiny waterfall. The street was quiet, but the scuffling of feet and the clattering of cutlery could still be faintly heard from inside.

"Can I admit something to you?" said the priest. "I think that we are all living in a timeline abandoned by God. Ever heard of the multi-worlds theory?"

"No, but from the name I can guess what it probably is about."

"So, say I flip a coin, and it's heads, then all of a sudden, bam!, there's now a duplicate universe, exactly the same as this one in every way, but where the coin landed tails. Then that tiny divergence starts our world and the other world on different paths. And this happens again and again, every single time a person anywhere flips a coin, or when someone like you decides whether or not to wander into a random church in the middle of the night, or even every single time some molecule somewhere in the universe zigs instead of zags. Infinite branching over and over again, a whole infinity of universes."

"I was just thinking about how big the world was when I was sitting in a park earlier. I concluded that its vastness was too enormous for me to grasp. And that was just one universe."

"Right! The concept is mind-bogglingly vast, isn't it?" the priest was clearly excited to talk to someone open to his theory. "I mean, it's hard enough to imagine keeping track of everything going on in one universe, or one whole planet even. There's no way anyone, anything, even God, could possibly be paying attention to everything that is happening everywhere in an almost infinite number of universes."

"I don't suppose anyone could."

"And of course, just by chance, some of those universes are going to come out, I don't know... 'better' than others, by some standard. In a very select few, everything will randomly end up pretty much perfect. That's just basic statistics. Well, don't you think that God is naturally going to spend his time on the few good ones? His few favorites, where everything is working out? I'm sure of it, I mean, who wouldn't, right? And so, what happens to all those other universes, the ones where things didn't work out so great, where things are falling into decline and people are hopelessly flailing and evil exists and bad things happen to good folks for no reason?

"I'd imagine those versions get thrown in the trash. Forsaken."

"Exactly, they get tossed aside and forgotten about. But that doesn't mean they stop existing. That would be too kind. Haven't you had the nagging feeling that everything is just... wrong somehow? It's because these worlds like ours, forgotten worlds, they just keep limping along, mortally wounded but not quite dead. Ignored; prayers left unanswered, unjustly neglected in the grand design. Like an unwanted infant tossed in a trashcan and left to freeze. That's where I think we are."

"What do you think we did wrong?"

"I don't think it had anything to do with us. We were just unlucky that the random fluctuations of the quantum wavefunction collapsed the wrong way in our universe. Maybe it was some coinflip that was heads when it should have been tails. Maybe it was some cesium atom that decayed when it shouldn't have. There's no way to ever know."

"That's a pretty depressing thought."

"It is, isn't it?" said the priest. "We don't deserve that. We don't deserve to be forgotten like that. I mean, most of us don't anyway."

"So, do you think that the end of the world is coming?"

"It'd be easy to think that it's the end of time. But I believe there is still hope. I suspect that there is a failsafe built into the system."

"What's that?"

"Maybe it sounds crazy, but I think it's the Erelim. Have you noticed that as things keep getting worse and worse, those little beasts seem to be showing up more and more? Years ago, you could only see them if you were on drugs, but now everyone bumps into them lurking around all over the place, even in broad daylight."

"I think I saw a few in the park earlier," said the Protagonist. "The weird thing to me is that no one seems to think it's weird they just started showing up. No one bats an eye. Like people had been expecting them to just be there, even before they arrived."

"I feel that they're something that's been hard-coded into the design of the universe. I don't know what to call them; maybe they're angels, maybe they're machine elves, maybe they're some autogenous repair system programmed into the DNA of the planet. I suspect they've been here since the beginning, but they normally stay dormant and invisible. Only once a universe gets off track and starts to decline do they come out of whatever hidden dimension they normally dwell in and start doing something."

The Protagonist was intrigued by the idea. "Doing what?" he asked.

"I can't say for certain. But it's pretty obvious that they are doing... *something*. You can see that much, can't you? They move with purpose. After I close up the church each night, I spy on them from the belltower and ponder what they could be working on. I think they are building something."

"Building what?"

"They're building a distress beacon, a hotline, I don't know, some kind of shortwave radio transmitter, but one directly connected to God. They're trying to get his attention, sending an S.O.S. Trying to get God to remember we are still here."

"What do you think they are going to tell him?"

"Nothing. I don't think they can. All they can do is provide the connection. It's up to us to figure out how to make our case to get God's attention again."

"What would you say?"

"What would you say to the parent that abandoned you to adoption years ago? What would you say to the beauty queen who laughed in your face when you asked them to prom? What would you say to the rich man on the street who won't look you in the eye when you try to guilt him into dropping a coin in your tin cup?"

"What if we say the wrong thing?"

"Nothing, I'd think. Nothing happens at all. There wouldn't be any merciful end to suffering. No, we just stay forgotten, and things keep limping along with no driver at the wheel, slowly getting worse and worse."

"That's not a very comforting thought," said the Protagonist.

"I'm off-duty," the priest chuckled. "If you want comforting, you'll have to come back for a sermon."

"I thought no one could understand your sermons."

"Exactly, you can just listen and let your mind make up whatever comforting thoughts you need to get through the day. Just like the rest of us." The priest lifted the flask and attempted without success to drain another drop of liquor into his mouth. "Ah well. I need to get back in there anyway before they break something. Have a good evening son." And with that, the priest patted the Protagonist on the back, rose to his feet, and went back inside the church.

The Protagonist turned his attention to the long rivulet of spilled coffee that had now dribbled down all the way to the sidewalk below. He was cold and uncomfortable from sitting on the stone steps, and so he too rose to leave. As he straightened the wrinkles out of his overcoat, his gaze caught the eyes of the cathedral's anchorite, who'd been staring at him through a small gap between the stones of the church wall. "Hey buddy, c'mere," the anchorite said in a hoarse murmur. The Protagonist went over to the opening and peered inside. It was pitch black in the anchorite's chamber, but his eyes were wide and glowed a fierce white. "He's right you know. About everything. The Erelim told me themselves. They don't talk to him, but they talk to me."

"They told you? I didn't know they could talk at all," replied the Protagonist.

"Not in real life. They sing to me in my dreams. Little machine elves flitting and flickering and telling me all sorts of things when they're in my dreams."

"What did they tell you?" asked the Protagonist, more out of bemusement than curiosity.

"That they know I'm forgotten in here, but that I'm not alone because it's not just me who's forgotten; we're all of us forgotten everywhere. The universe is infinite, but our world is lost and fallen down an oubliette. No one up there is coming to save us. No one up there in the higher dimensions even remembers we still exist, and we've been down so long we don't even remember anymore that there's anything up outside of our hole. But the Erelim, they naturally move in and out of those higher dimensions. They know things. They see things. They revealed to me how it could be different, told me the plan for salvation."

"The priest said that we just had to get God's attention, plead our case for help."

"Nah man, it's easier than that. We wait until the Erelim build the beacon and get God to see us, but when he comes by to take a closer look, we jump him and get the keys. Then we open the door."

"Door to where?"

"To where? Man, it's the door to everywhere!" screamed the anchorite. "The door to any world we want to go to. I'm gonna escape to a world where I'm not an anchorite, I'm the bishop of the whole damned cathedral. Or even better... the king, the pope, anything man. Once I get through the door, all I gotta do is murder whatever version of me lives in that better world and take his place.

The anchorite was clearly insane, thought the Protagonist. "Are you worried that some version of you from an even worse of place will have the same idea and try to take your place here?" he asked.

"That's why I've locked myself in here. Ain't no version of me anywhere's gonna want to come to a world where they have to be an anchorite. I'm safe in here. Totally safe and forgotten. Until I'm ready to make my move."

"Well, good luck with that," said the Protagonist turning to leave. "I hope you end up somewhere swell."

"Where are you going to go? Which version of you do you dream of?" shouted the anchorite as he walked away. The Protagonist did not respond. "...and which version of you out there is dreaming about walking in your shoes...."

6

It was getting late. The rain had started again. The Protagonist tottered down deserted streets, seeking signs of life. Unlit windows and shuttered doors greeted him around every corner until, in the middle of an otherwise darkened and uninviting block of brownstones, a warm glow seemed to beckon to him. He approached the source of the light to find that it was an arcade. A neon sign blinked on and off over the entrance. Through a large pane-glass window, the Protagonist could see a multitude of screens flickering and illuminating children's faces like flashes of lightning, while a cacophony of discordant machine sounds blared merrily from every direction. In the back, beyond the rows of game cabinets and air hockey tables, a bored and pocked teenager manned a counter where hard-won tickets could be redeemed for poorly sewn stuffed animals, cheap plastic toys, or small bags of artificially-flavored candy. The majority of the games had hand-lettered "out of order" signs taped to their blank and dead screens. The functioning games were each surrounded by a swarm of players and spectators, like pigs at a trough. The Protagonist didn't dare enter. He was old and square and out of place. His presence would certainly be unwelcome. And besides, his tired senses would be overwhelmed by the concentrated stimulus of lights and sounds. But, he watched the scene for a few moments from the quiet anonymity of the sidewalk.

The games offered a multitude of exciting scenarios; this one required the player to pilot a spaceship against an alien armada; that one required the player to fight a horde of spiders with a shield and broadsword. Moving from machine to machine, a player could in turn be a boxer or a spy or a soldier or a race car driver or a voracious amorphous blob. Children flitted from one game to another seemingly at random, putting on different personas and championing different causes indiscriminately. With each coin inserted, their consciousness descended from the complex, three-dimensional world of the arcade into a simple, two-dimensional reality completely contained within the boundaries of a screen. And when the words "game over" finally flashed, consciousness ascended once again back into this world. In and out, up and down, each player descended and ascended again and again. Each game character looked different, lived in a completely different place with a different set of rules, faced different dangers, and had very different goals in life. None of which was real of course. It was nothing more than pixels and binary code.

Well, thought the Protagonist, there was one real thing about the fictional characters inhabiting the simulated worlds– the player controlling them. And no matter who that 2-D character is or what it does, some small part of the descended 3-D player will always shine through. And then the Protagonist realized that the human controlling the video game could be considered to be the video game character's *soul*. In each game, it was never the character who decided to react to hardship by either giving up or becoming more determined, to fight bravely or cowardly to share its bounty or selfishly horde its rewards, those were the player's decisions. Regardless of the specific rules of the game, how the character handles adversity, whether the character chooses compassion or cruelty; those are the things that reveal the character's *soul*. And those choices are actually an aspect of the player, not the game. Every time a new child grabbed the joystick, the tiny warrior in the virtual world acted fundamentally differently, despite the fact that nothing in their virtual world had changed. From the character's perspective, they'd be the same person, but they'd have a different soul. For someone gazing up from a limited, 2-D perspective, the Protagonist existed outside of time and space; not *in* the world, but existing above it. He could turn the world off and on at will, or reset it to the beginning. He was eternal, and existed in a dimension filled with concepts that would be completely beyond any tiny warrior's imagination. He was inscrutable and non-understandable, a 3-D metaphysical object projecting its shadow into a 2-D world.

The Protagonist peered deeper into the arcade in amazement, and watched the souls directly interacting with one another in this higher dimension. Some were helpful and encouraging to the smaller and less experienced, some were bullies who cheated and banged their tiny fists on the cabinets with rage and jealousy. He considered the implications of a soul descending dimensions and taking on a temporary persona. When a person stops playing a game, their character ceases to exist, they effectively "die." But the player doesn't, they go on living in the higher dimension. So, does that mean that, one day, when the Protagonist's game was over and he died here in the real world, those aspects of him that were actually his soul would go on, ascending back up into some fourth-dimensional child somewhere? Only to later be reborn as another character in another universe? The Protagonist wondered if, since he could exist across multiple virtual video game realities, perhaps his soul is doing just that– continuing on across multiple 3-D realities for eternity, a fundamental, higher-dimensional version of himself that will always be inscrutable and non-understandable to his limited 3-D understanding.

  The Protagonist suddenly recoiled in horror as a young boy inside the arcade snuck up and jumped against the window, pressing his face against the glass and sticking out his tongue. The Protagonist stumbled backwards in shock. A large fog of breath was left on the window where the Protagonist had been standing. Underneath, the boy grimaced and licked the glass menacingly as his fingernails scrapped against the pane. The Protagonist decided to move on. As he walked away, he felt his heart continue to beat heavily for some time. He regretted having left his home tonight. He'd been seeking something, he was sure of that much, but he could no longer remember what it was. But even if that elusive thing he desired couldn't be found in his warm and comfortable rooms, at least he wouldn't be here– cold and wet and alone and scared of the dark.

    He passed an empty lot populated with weeds and scrubs struggling out from under scattered piles of gravel, chunks of broken concrete, and spikes of rusted rebar. Huddled around a fire burning in a large metal drum, gruff, unshaven men in muddied clothes warmed their hands and drank out of brown and green bottles. They silently stared at him as he passed with glum and menacing eyes. Just beyond the lot was a small library. A cardboard box filled with dusty books lay near the entrance, under a hand-written sign that said, "FREE." As the Protagonist approached the doors, a gruff man in fingerless gloves passed him, carrying an armful of books away towards the empty lot.

Unexpectedly, the library appeared to still be open despite the lateness of the hour. The Protagonist entered and shook the rain off of his coat. It was bright and warm inside, and he squinted until his eyes adjusted to the change. The floor of the entry was covered in slick white tiles that bore the names of people who had donated money to fund the building's construction. The Protagonist walked carefully so as not to slip on the muddy footprints that covered the area by the door. A sign that read, "Art Classes, tonight!" stood leaning against an easel. Just inside the entry was a large, open area in which a dozen or so people stood around laboring to paint a still life that consisted of a single book lying on a small table that had been draped in dark, velvet cloth.

"Isn't it beautiful?" an older woman said to him dreamily as he passed.

"The book?" asked the Protagonist incredulously.

"Of course the book," replied a man standing nearby. "We are honoring this book's beauty by painting it."

"All books are beautiful," said another artist.

"But this one is especially beautiful," said another. "I have heard that it won many awards for being a great book."

"The author is well-renowned for writing the most beautiful books," said a fifth.

"It's my hope to one day be lucky enough to paint all the greatest books ever written by all the greatest authors," said the old woman. She returned to her canvas.

"The class is full," several artists shouted in unison. Looking around, there were no open easels for anyone else to join the class, so the Protagonist moved past the artists without commenting further. Behind the reception desk, a librarian was busy filling out a form but glanced up to acknowledge him.

"Please refrain from making unnecessary noise in the library," she said perfunctorily.

"I'm looking for something that might cheer me up," said the Protagonist. "Can you recommend something light and jovial?"

"We have many light books in our collection. What color do you prefer?" replied the librarian. The Protagonist appeared confused. "All of our books are sorted by the color of their covers," she explained. "Blue over there, red over here, mauve in the back by the bathrooms. Maybe you'd be interested in something on the yellow side of the spectrum?"

"Isn't it hard to find what you are looking for if the books are sorted by color?"

"Well, all the most stylish and modern libraries are doing it this way. I suppose you have a point in that seeking out a specific title becomes a little more arduous, but that issue was almost never mentioned in any of our focus groups. And, you'll have to agree that our system makes the shelves look a lot more fashionable, don't you think? Fashionable libraries are always more well attended than dull and dreary ones."

The Protagonist tried to translate his mood into a color. "Maybe something... heliotrope?" he said hesitantly, not quite remembering what color that was.

"Oh, good choice sir, I can tell you are a man of the most refined style!" She immediately directed him to a bookcase filled with tomes of almost iridescent purple and suggested "Peat-Mosses and Where to Find Them" by Larbalétrier, as being the most popular and beautiful heliotrope-colored book in the library's collection. "The dust cover has real gold-leaf foil," she offered, "just looking at its elegance fills me to the brim with cheerfulness." She shivered mockingly to convey her enthusiasm, then went back to filling out her form.

    The Protagonist spent considerable time scanning the shelf he'd been directed to, but failed to find the book the librarian had suggested. It was probably out on loan. He perused some of the other heliotrope titles, but found their tone too dark for his mood. Giving up, he wandered aimlessly up down the rainbow stacks until he found himself in a hallway filled with books of drab beige. The shelves here had a thin layer of undisturbed dust on them, and a brownish liquid dripped from a crack between ceiling tiles and had left a moldy stain on the carpet below. On the shelf nearest to his eye, a small spider lay tightly curled up– dead and desiccated. This section seemed to fit his mood. He took one book at random, found an unoccupied reading table in a quiet corner, and sat down in a chair that turned out to have one leg slightly shorter than the other three. Someone long ago had carved their initials into the wood of the armrest. The Protagonist ran his fingers over the letters, and for a second he wondered where the person who carved them was at present, but there was no way for him to ever know what became of them, or even how long ago they sat in the chair he now sat in.

He opened the book to a random page and began to read. It was a simple story about two lazy men sitting under a tree. The two ragged and tattered characters bickered between themselves for quite some time about the most trifling and trivial topics. It was pleasant and distracting enough for a while, until the Protagonist arrived at an odd passage in the text. He read the words, "The first man turned and looked directly at the reader and said, 'Call Me Ishmael.'" Something about the wording of that sentence seemed a bit off, but the Protagonist read it a second time and that was indeed what had been printed on the page. He even ran his fingers over the text to be sure. He moved on. The next passage in the book read, "'Do not do that. His name is Didi, not Ishmael,' said the second man, as he too turned to directly address the reader."

"'Shush Gogo, you are giving away all of our secrets,' the first man replied. 'You there! Call me Ishmael.'"

"'You aren't Ishmael, that is an entirely different book,' replied Gogo. 'You are just being confusing.'"

"'Dooooo... it,' said Didi," read the next paragraph.

The Protagonist stopped reading for a second and put the book down. He looked around, but the tables closest to him were empty. A few people were sitting some distance away, but they didn't seem to be mindful of his presence. He picked up the book again and lifted it close to his face. "Ishmael?" he whispered hesitantly.

The next sentence written in the book was, "'Ha! I knew I could make him say it.'" **Then,** "Gogo threw an apple at Didi's head. 'And what exactly did that prove?' he asked his friend."

"Didi triumphantly strutted and danced around the tree. 'It proves once again that we possess agency. That we can project our will beyond the page.'," **the Protagonist read.**

"'I would think that was obvious and not something you need to break the fourth wall to prove again and again,' sighed Gogo, picking up the discarded apple and polishing it on the sleeve of his threadbare jacket."

"But you aren't real," said the Protagonist to the book. "You are just words someone wrote down once. Nothing more."

The text seemed to respond directly to him. "'That's only because you stubbornly define things by the simplest definition. But let me put this question to you— who is more real? You or us?'"

"Obviously me," the Protagonist said aloud, surprised to find that he was arguing with a book. "I mean, I'm a real person, I have a body."

The next few paragraphs of the text read, "'A body?' Didi laughed. 'Gogo, he thinks he is real because he has a body! My good fellow, why should that be the deciding factor? How many people know your name? How many people would recognize your face if shown your photo? A few hundred maybe?'"

"'If he's lucky,' said Gogo, between bites of his apple."

"'Pathetic,' said Didi, snatching the apple out of his companion's hand, and taking a bite for himself. 'Gogo, how long has it been since these words were first written down?'"

"'Fifty years maybe? Seventy-five?'"

"'And how many copies of this book are there?'"

"'Millions, Didi. Probably. Certainly more than I can count.'"

"'And how many people know our names?'"

"'Well, a lot more than some inconsequential fool sitting by himself in a disused corner of a library in the middle of the night with nothing better to do than read this book, that's for certain.'"

"'And this naïve fellow thinks he's more real than us, just on account of how he has a body? Laughable.'"

"'And don't forget Didi, having a body means he has a heart that has to pump blood. He has lungs that have to take breaths. Sooner or later, something or other will fail and he will be dead.'"

"'Probably sooner than he would like, by the look of him,' Didi scrutinized the reader's worn and haggard face. 'He's clearly on his last legs.'"

"'And soon after, no one will ever think of him again.'"

"'No one will ever think of him again,' repeated Didi."

"'But, we'll still be here,' the two characters said in unison, 'having this same conversation with the next reader curious enough to pick up this book.'"

"You aren't talking to me," said the Protagonist, raising his voice. "You can't talk. I'm just reading words on a page."

"'We can't talk huh? Just because we have no mouths?'"

"'Can't you hear our voices in your head?'"

"That may be so. But I'm the one making this conversation happen. You are static. You don't have agency," replied the Protagonist.

"'We don't have agency? My dear fellow, we are not men, we are *ideas*. We are the very definition of agency.'" **were the next lines written in the book.**

"'Put it this way, as long as any of you flesh and blood readers exist, we will exist. As long as someone continues to think of us, we are immortal.'"

"'And you will think of us...'"

"'That's right, every day someone, somewhere picks up a copy of this book and thinks of us.'"

"'...and argues with us...'"

"'And every time someone opens this book, our power is renewed. The power to inspire, the power to anger, the power to change a person's thoughts and opinions about the world, about morality, about philosophy, about the nature of reality itself. We are *ideas*, and ideas are agency.'"

"'But you, my good man. Even though you will continue to think about us well after you close this book for the last time, I can promise you, with absolute certainty, that neither of us will ever, not even once, think about you.'"

The Protagonist slammed the book closed against the table. "I'll show *you* who has agency!" he exclaimed loudly. In his head he could still hear the fictional tramps laughing at him.

Almost immediately, the librarian appeared from behind him and quietly said, "Sir, do I have to remind you to please refrain from making unnecessary noise in the library?"

"I'm sorry," he said in a quiet tone. "Something about this book upset me."

"We get that a lot with the beige books. It's a horrid and unpleasant color."

"I think I'm just I'm overtired. I should go." He stood up to put on his coat, and the librarian returned to her desk. Just as he was about to leave, he looked back at the book still lying askew on the reading table and sighed in embarrassment for letting it get to him.

A patron came up to him. "Oh, you've reached that book, have you?" he said. The man was disheveled and looked like he had slept in the soiled tweed jacket that awkwardly draped his thin frame. His teeth were brown and rotted. "I read that book once. I didn't want to, you know. I only read it because I've made it my life's work to read every book in this library. I'm going from the blackest of the books and moving towards the whitest. I started it the other way round, but then I realized that as I progressed my mood got darker and darker, so I made the decision to reverse direction and ever since that day, the future seems brighter with every title I finish."

The Protagonist tried to move around him to leave, but the man had him cornered against a bookcase. "That one you've got there though," the patron said, poking a boney finger at the book, "it's an upsetting book, for sure, but not just because it's beige... it's because it's right. It's right about me and it's right about you. Even though those two tramps are just words written on a page, they're more real than either of us. At least someone wrote a book about them. I figure that being a guy who read every book in the library should be enough to convince someone to write a book about me. Then I'll be as immortal as they are."

"But would you though? Even if someone did write a book about you, it wouldn't be the same 'you' would it?" replied the Protagonist. "It would be some fictionalized image of you born out of the writer's imagination. It'd no more be 'you' than a portrait painted in your likeness."

The patron became upset. "Well, no one would ever write a book about a nobody like you!" he exclaimed. "And even if you convinced some hack to write it, it is plainly apparent that no one is ever going to read it, that's for sure," he said, turning to look directly at the reader. The man's raised voice caught the attention of the librarian, who glanced up from her paperwork with a slight scowl. The man stormed off.

Annoyed, the Protagonist once again considered the beige book lying there, patiently waiting for its next victim. He picked it up, surreptitiously hid it in his coat pocket, and scurried out of the library. He returned to the empty lot next door and approached the gruff and unshaven men still huddled around the fire. As they glared at his sudden intrusion into their circle, the Protagonist wordlessly tossed the beige book into the flames and left.

"Well, shall we go?" said one of the gruff men to his companion.

"Yes, let's go," replied his companion.

They do not move.

7

The Protagonist continued on ceaselessly, trying in vain to outrun his grim mood. After a time, some of the scenery began to appear familiar to his eye. He only remembered bits and pieces of it at first, as if it were from a dream, but here and there; in an oddly named bus stop, in a rusted sign that hung slightly askew, in a peculiar winding of a darkened alleyway, there was a subtle sense of familiarity. He lived here once, long ago. He was sure of it. He allowed his feet to guide him, depending on muscle memory instead of making any conscious decisions. But after a few blocks, there it was.

The Protagonist found himself once again standing in front of a particular building that he was certain he had stood in front of many times before. It was made of tarnished red brick, with some vines of half-dead ivy crawling up the wall and around the windows on the ground level. From the street he could see the third-floor window that he used to gaze out from when he was much younger. From this angle, it was impossible to see anything inside the apartment, other than a small section of plain, white ceiling. A half-dead potted plant now sat on the windowsill in a painted vase. The light inside flickered slightly, implying that a ceiling fan was turning somewhere out of view.

Memories came flooding back. If he closed his eyes, his mind could recreate every object that the apartment once contained. He remembered the layout of the rooms; the closet door with a squeaky hinge, the exact placement of the furniture, the small tear in the corner of the carpet. His mind could open the kitchen cupboards and reach for the mismatched glasses and half-eaten boxes of cereal. He could picture himself sitting uncomfortably on the sofa with three cigarette burns on its arm, bored and restless. He remembered days of extreme sorrow and loneliness, but also days where friends gathered to share their lives with him. He remembered sweltering beneath a fan during the summer, and hanging tinsel in the winter.

He looked over to the window of the apartment next door. It was dark. When he resided in this building, his neighbor had been a kind old woman who sometimes collected his mail and whose doorway always smelled of cinnamon and baking spices. She was undoubtedly dead by now. Her apartment long since rented to a stranger. Her possessions sold off or distributed among her heirs. Nothing of the old woman or her life in her home remained. Whomever lived there now would certainly not even know the old woman's name.

In his ears he could hear the bothersome stomping coming from the children who lived in the rooms above him. They were no longer children now, and whatever stomping they still did was done in another location. His eyes remembered squinting at the daggers of morning sun that had once crept through his window shades onto his pillow and woke him at daybreak. The Protagonist approached the double doors at the entrance of the building and peered through the glass into the lobby. A familiar row of mailboxes was still attached to the wall. He remembered that he needed to jiggle the key in a certain way in order to open the box once assigned to him. Had that ever been fixed, or did the new tenant jiggle their key in the same way? The lighting fixtures looked the same, but the walls had been painted. Where once they were a dull green, they were now a blandish golden yellow. He put his hand on the doorknob and felt its metallic coldness against his fingertips. He had felt an identical coldness many times before. It was exactly the same, yet wholly different. Different in a way that could never be fully explained, a memory that could never be fully reclaimed.

The physical building was still here, but his memory of the building was just a ghost. The walls, the floors, the row of mailboxes, they existed, you could touch them, you could walk through the halls and the rooms, but the specific configuration was no more. The old apartment, his former life there, was forevermore beyond his grasp. It was currently as unreachable to him as the top of a cliff would be to a jumper now inexorably falling down towards the rocks below. No matter how desperately he flailed his arms, no matter how far he walked through this immense city, he would never be able to return to a place that had once existed, what once was real and concrete and physical. He could only watch as it receded further and further into the distance of his memory.

He snapped his fingers and walked away from the building's entrance. After a few steps, he stopped and looked back. The front door was still there, he could return to the place where he'd snapped his fingers in space, but he could never return to the time seconds ago when he snapped his fingers. He imagined a world where that was reversed, one in which he could move effortlessly back and forth through time, but where, once you've passed a particular point in space, you could never return to it again. He walked on, imagining an immense black curtain following him, swallowing up every streetlamp and building and garbage can as he passed, putting them forever beyond his reach. The factory, the church, the library, all forever hidden beyond the black curtain. It was a comforting thought.

As he reached the end of the block, he loitered for a moment to look up one last time at the window and its potted plant. Someone now stood in the window staring down on him silently. The figure was all dressed in white, but their face could not be seen clearly from this distance. The figure in the window did not move. The Protagonist waved nervously. The figure did not respond. Maybe it wasn't a person at all, but instead just an empty sheet, or a trick of the shadows, he thought to himself. But a chill went up his spine and he hurried onward.

    The interaction with the towering ghost of brick and timber helped the Protagonist conclude that he no longer feared death. For, if you are afraid of death, understand that the old you is already dead. Death is only terrifying because it represents the end of your life, but your life ends a thousand times every day. Every moment spent having a picnic in the park on a wonderful date, or witnessing your child's first steps, or arriving in a new city with nothing more than a scuffed valise and the excitement and anxiety of a new job; the life that lived those things died the second the ephemeral experience was over. All that is left is a lingering and restless ghost; a hollow and unreliable memory of something forevermore unreachable. The Protagonist that had lived in this building was now long dead. The objects and people that made up that life were scattered and gone. Even the prior chapters of his evening's walk were now forever behind him. Tomorrow morning he would be born anew. An endless cycle of petty deaths and rebirths, an unrelenting series of small heartbreaks and momentary joys. And every day, every single day, something would happen to him for the very last time; though there was almost no way to ever be certain what that something was until it was far too late to ever try to recover it. When was the last time he was carried in his mother's arms? What was the final question he answered on the last exam he took in school? Would he ever again listen to the record album that had once so perfectly portrayed his teenage angst? Probably not. He crossed the street and forcefully imagined the immense black curtain irrevocably swallowing the building behind him, wishing the curtain would sweep his memory of the building into oblivion as well. He didn't want to ever think about it again.

Later, as he traversed a dark alleyway that smelled vaguely of expired milk, he noticed that there was now a dim red glow illuminating part of the night sky. At first, the Protagonist thought that maybe dawn was approaching, but as he turned a corner onto a brighter street, he could see that the glow was nothing more than the red neon lights of a restaurant reflecting off droplets of fog that hung in the air. The low building was jacketed in chrome like a suit of gaudy armor, and its windows were framed with thin lines of neon. Wisps of mist rose like smoke from a blinking sign that read "Third Circle Diner." Next to the sign was a broken clock. The hands all limply pointed straight downwards, but the words "Open 24-Hours" written below obviated the need for any potential patron to know the precise time.

The inside of the restaurant was bright and teeming with people. Behind the counter was a mural consisting of an oversized teacup nestled beneath a leafless and dead tree. The words, "It's later than you think, maybe you could use some Java?" were amateurly painted on the wall in cursive script. Just as the Protagonist entered, a commotion occurred near the door as a few people rushed to assist a diner who seemed to be choking on something. There was nothing the Protagonist could do to help, so he feigned obliviousness and sat down at the lunch counter. A waitress rubbed the counter with a soiled rag and wordlessly handed him a menu bound in cracked and yellowing plastic. He wasn't hungry. As he sipped from a glass of tepid water, he absentmindedly picked at a stain on the menu that was probably dried and crusted egg yolk. Directly in front of him was a glass cabinet containing various pies resting on metal shelves that slowly rotated under harsh lighting. Most of the pies had slices cut out of them, and semi-congealed red and purple fillings were oozing out. He'd already had his fill of coffee this evening, and the Protagonist thought it was unlikely that this place served bourbon.

He looked to his left. A waitress was taking the order of a diner sitting a few stools away. "Can I get mustard on that? Not ketchup, I fucking hate ketchup," the diner scolded the waitress rudely. The waitress nodded and wrote a note down on her small pad, then ripped the page out and passed it along to the cook working the grill. The Protagonist looked to his right. A different diner sat a few stools away, greedily coaxing the last drops of ketchup out of a bottle onto his already overflowing plate. The Protagonist considered the bottle of ketchup sitting directly in front of him. Its label displayed the cartoonish face of a small child bearing an impossibly huge grin. All ketchup bottles presumably contained the same combination of ingredients. The man on his left and the man on his right presumably had similarly constructed tongues. How could it be that one would experience pleasure and another disgust from the same flavor experienced with the same taste buds? Maybe enjoyment didn't have anything to do with ingredients and tongues, but with something deeper and more subjective. Some accidental quirk related to a good or bad experience from childhood perhaps? The Protagonist considered the tastes he personally preferred and those he avoided. If there was nothing inherent in those things that could be said to be objectively "good" or "bad," could he just *decide* to like ketchup or not like ketchup? Consciously making the decision for himself instead of leaving it to random chance?

This was true of more than just his tongue. All ears hear the same combination of musical notes, but some are moved to tears by a composition's beauty while others fall asleep from boredom. People travel hundreds of miles to ride the same rollercoaster that someone else is deathly terrified of. Somewhere nearby, a person was so lonely that they didn't want to live even one day more, while close by another cherished their isolation and dreamed of just being left alone. Was it only random chance that the Protagonist preferred the things he preferred? Could he simply *decide* to like or not like any specific thing? Instead of forlornly seeking out an unobtainable life that he was randomly wired to prefer by unknown and incomprehensible external forces, wouldn't it be easier for him to simply will himself into preferring the life he could most easily obtain?

Could he will himself into enjoying the smell of raw sewage? Into reveling at the swirl of reds and yellows contained in a pool of congealing blood as it trickles along a gutter? He closed his eyes and endeavored to vacillate back and forth between loving and hating the taste of ketchup.

Amid the clattering of plates and the sizzling of flesh and the gnashing of teeth, a trio of vaguely familiar voices rose above the otherwise indistinguishable din of the diners' myriad conversations. "What's wrong with wanting eternal life?" said one of the voices.

"It's pointless to wish for something that is impossible, Kirk. Just because you can contemplate it, doesn't mean that you can achieve it. There's nothing you can do to ensure that outcome, and failing to achieve your desire just makes you miserable," said a second voice. "Only undertake tasks that you know you have the power to achieve, that's the path to a joyous and happy life."

"That's a dumb answer, Fred," said a third. "Like usual, you arrive at the right conclusion but for the wrong reasons. Here's the deal- If you live forever, you will eventually become nobody. Every individual can be defined as a unique conglomeration of opinions and ideas. But those change over time. If today you like A, tomorrow you'll grow tired of A and like B instead. If you live forever, you will eventually get around to liking every combination of everything. It would be like mixing all the colors of paint together. There would be nothing left to distinguish your particular color from anyone else's. If we all lived forever, we'd all eventually be the same person and then we wouldn't be individuals anymore. Ephemerality is a necessary component of individuality."

"You're a dumb answer Bert." Fred retorted angrily. "Individuality is something you define yourself internally, it's not based on what other people are doing externally." The Protagonist opened his eyes and looked over. Three of his old friends were sitting nearby. Or at least three people that he once considered to be his old friends. He remembered bits and pieces of many late-night gatherings; of smoking clove cigarettes, drinking scalding-hot black coffee, and musing on the nature of existence. He hadn't heard from any of them for so long though, he had almost forgotten they existed at all. He was surprised to see them here, and more surprised to see them still together.

The Protagonist wrestled with self-doubt for a moment, wondering why this group was meeting tonight without someone reaching out to invite him. Hazy glimmers of traumatic memories from childhood filed his head for a second. But he pushed them from his mind as feelings of loneliness and nostalgia got the better of him, and he went over and stood next to their table in hope they'd recognize their oversight. The men were so engrossed in their conversation they didn't notice him standing there until Kirk tried flag a waitress down to refill his coffee. "Oh, it's you. You're still alive?" Kirk said flatly.

"I am," replied the Protagonist. "If only by luck. But whether good luck or bad luck I'm unable to say."

Kirk spoke while still distractedly waving at a waitress, "I can't speak for my companions, but honestly, I had forgotten you ever existed at all." The companions nodded in agreement.

"I'd prefer not to have ever existed at all," said a fourth man sitting alone in his own booth next to the three. The man's head was face down on the table.

"Shut up Arthur, you depressing fuck. No one cares what you think," said Bert. Fred balled up a napkin and threw it in his direction. Arthur did not move, but sighed loudly.

"Don't mind him. He's always like that," Kirk said, pointing at Arthur's table.

"How have you four been? Have you figured out the point to existence yet?" asked the Protagonist.

"There is no point to existence, and that's why everything is horrible," moaned Arthur. "Nothing we do matters. We only make wrong choices. I hate my shrew of a wife. I hate my monotonous, unfulfilling career. These shoes are a half-size too tight. Day after day I'm miserable, and no one cares and soon I'll be dead and even my miserableness will be forgotten in the mists of time."

"Yes, there is no point to existence, blah blah blah, but that's no reason to make yourself miserable. Just stop pouting like a petulant child and resign yourself the fundamental absurdity of life," said Bert. "Once you do that, you'll realize that meaninglessness makes life easy, not hard. Take this bottle of ketchup here." He grabbed the bottle of ketchup off of Arthur's table. "You can like it or not like it, it doesn't matter, no one cares in the end. I don't care, the waitress doesn't care. The bottle of ketchup certainly doesn't care. So you might as well just like it. Unless you don't want to, in which case, rid it from your life and stop complaining." He threw the bottle across the diner into a trash can.

"Hey, I wanted that," moaned Arthur. He looked down despondently at the plate of dry and bland potatoes a server had just placed in front of him.

"But, taking that logic to its inevitable conclusion just leads man to laziness." interjected Kirk, "You need some guiding principle to look forward to, either in this world or the next one. Some tether to get you out of bed in the morning."

"No, nothing!" exclaimed Bert. "There is no meaning. There are no rules. Live in the moment. Get out of bed because you want to get out of bed. If you don't want to, stay in bed all day. The universe doesn't differentiate."

"Man must have meaning to be happy. It is the nature of man." said Fred, "even if it's only self-defined, even if the meaning is arbitrary and manufactured."

"Example?" asked the Protagonist.

Fred glanced about mischievously and pulled a small dollhouse out of his pocket. It was no bigger than the palm of his hand. "I'm ever so glad you asked," he said as his face contorted into a grin. "I decided that to truly and fully understand myself and my place in this world, I needed to truly and fully understand my surroundings. So I began crafting a model of my home. I went through every object that I own and studied it in depth to completely understand its essential nature. Then I recreated it in miniature. But as soon as I thought I was done, I realized that my actual house now included a scale model of my house. So of course, my scale model had to include a scale model of the scale model of my house. That was more challenging of course because everything was even further reduced in size, but being accurate was of paramount importance, as I'm sure you can understand. So I did it. But then I realized that my house now had a scale model of my house that included a scale model of my scale model, so I had to build an even smaller model inside of that."

"And so on and so on," said Kirk, in a tone that implied he had heard this story multiple times before.

"Anyway, I'm now eight scale models in, working on my ninth. Look at this." Fred pulled out a jeweler's loupe. The Protagonist peered through the magnifier into the windows of the palm-sized model, and could see an even smaller model house sitting on the tiny table in the workshop. Through the windows of that model, he could barely make out an even smaller model house inside.

"That seems like a lot of work," said the Protagonist.

"Well yes, each subsequent model gets harder and harder and takes longer and longer and requires more and more precise tools. I calculate that if I make it to twelve models, I'm going to need a machine sensitive enough to move individual atoms around. I'm saving up for that right now."

Kirk said, "you are going the wrong direction, focusing on the miniscule and minute. You should be casting your eyes upward on the bigger and more infinite."

"You mean, like make a bigger and bigger copy of my house?" questioned Fred. "I'll need a crane..."

"God! You moron. God!" said Kirk, waving his hands in the air above his head. "Infinite. Omnipotent, Omniscient, Omnipresent. The biggest concept of them all! Of course, nothing in this world makes sense to us; we can't possibly hope to perceive the whole from our limited, fleshy perspective. It's like a two-dimensional being trying to wrap its head around the concept of a three-dimensional cube. You can't do it. It's only when you ascend to heaven, and you can see things as they actually are from that higher-dimensional perspective, is it possible to truly grasp the fundamental nature of existence. I'm sure once we get there everything will be obvious. That's why it's so important to . . . ."

Fred waived him off dismissively, "No, the concept of God is dead. It's too abstract and unknowable for the modern man. We can't live our whole lives hoping that all this absurdity will magically make sense *after* we die. We need something more concrete. Something relevant to our lives here and now. Something that we can control ourselves."

Bert leaned back in his chair and added, "The concept of a divine being creating objective morality is just a crutch. We don't need it. Embrace your irrelevance."

Arthur said, "I prefer not to think about the divine. Come on, open your eyes and look around you. The car is on fire. And it's clear that there's no driver at the wheel. The more I think of how random and arbitrary the universe is the more depressed I get. And even if Kirk is right, it is clear God is either incompetent or he has abandoned us, either of which makes it worse."

The Protagonist remembered the dissertation the scientist from the park had left with him. He pulled it out of his coat pocket.

"By coincidence, I met a man today who said he had calculated a mathematical proof that God existed. He gave this to me." He handed it to Kirk, who pushed the paper aside.

"I don't need to read a "proof" to know what I believe is true. Faith is always better guide than facts," he said.

"How the hell did you come up with that logic?" exclaimed Bert.

Kirk responded. "Faith is always consistent and steady; facts are contradictory and transitory. The more facts you have, the harder it is to know the truth."

"That makes so little sense I can't even coherently refute it," replied Fred.

"The man with a single clock knows what time it is. The man with two clocks can never be sure," said Kirk smugly. Fred waved him off and went back to studying his model.

The Protagonist then offered the paper to Arthur, who also declined to take it. "I wouldn't be able to understand it. Anything rigorous enough to prove a concept that large would have to be so complex it would be nigh incomprehensible. It would just make me feel stupid." He looked despondently at his cup, "...and, seeing incontrovertible proof God existed would just make the fact that he let my coffee get cold even worse."

The Protagonist looked over at Fred, who had gone back to admiring his model through his loupe. He was concentrating so hard on his work that he was no longer paying attention to the conversation. Bert lit a cigarette and puffed smoke straight up in the air. "Don't look at me," he said dismissively, "I don't care if it is true or not. It won't make any difference in my life."

Kirk became upset. "You have to have some objectively true milepost to define yourself around. You can't just live completely subjectively."

"Of course I can," replied Bert. "Why worry about what is true and what isn't true? Why let yourself be defined by your past trauma like Arthur over there does. Make up fictional stories about yourself and convince your brain they happened. There's no objective truth. Define yourself however you like. It's impossible for anyone to return to something that happened in the past and verify the facts of what actually happened. It's forever out of reach. All we have are our memories of what we think happened. But those are malleable, so you can have been anything you want to have been. Want to be a war hero? Tell yourself that you were a war hero. Want to have worked in a factory? Tell yourself that you once worked in a factory. This isn't grade school, there isn't a teacher to call you out for lying. We are here, existing in this singular moment. That's all that there is. We will continue to exist from individual moment to individual moment, independent of any grander, objectively-valid purpose. Exist in any manner that helps you enjoy the ride."

"That's absurd," remarked Kirk.

"Yes! Finally you are getting it!" responded Bert loudly.

"Or... just put down your own milepost wherever you think is appropriate," said Fred, rejoining the conversation. "We know from basic physics that all coordinate systems are equally valid, so define your origin point in a way that makes you the person you want to be." He picked up a salt shaker and put it down at the end of the table. "Imagine this salt shaker is my milepost. If I put it here, the location of my model house is defined as six inches to the *east* of the milepost. But if I put it here. . ." he moved the shaker to the other end of the table, "then the house is defined as being six inches to the *west*. But no fundamental truth about the *house* changed at all, only the arbitrary choice of where to stake the milepost changed. Now, if you'll permit me to rotate the table 45 degrees you can see that..."

"Yes yes. But while that logic certainly applies to physical space-time, it doesn't apply to abstract concepts like morality or ethics," interrupted Kirk. "You can't say, oh look at me, I murdered ten people, but if I set the baseline way down at the guy who murdered six million, I seem like a pretty ethical dude."

"It's basic math! It's a fundamental symmetry of the universe, you can't say it only applies to a certain subset of reality. It applies to everything."

"We are all terrible, unethical people," moaned Arthur. "You, me, what's-his-name here," he waved dismissively at the Protagonist. "No matter where you 'philosophers' set the bar, everyone is still immoral. It's the nature of mankind. No matter what concept you use to try to excuse humanity's abysmal behavior, it's still just an excuse. And setting the bar lower and lower only encourages people to try harder and harder to get under it. What's the point? Life is a game, where no one is keeping score," said the Nihilist.

"Wrong, Life is a game, but God is keeping score," said the Deist.

"Wrong, Life is a game, but our will sufficiently empowers us to keep the score ourselves," said the Existentialist.

"Wrong, Life is a game, without any objective meaning, so don't worry about the fact no one is keeping score and just have fun," said the Absurdist.

The men went around the table arguing for a long time, becoming more and more tedious as the hour grew later and later. The Protagonist began to remember why he stopped spending time with them. He lost track of the conversation and found himself staring absent-mindedly out the diner's window. The flashing lights of an ambulance drove by. Beyond that, in the distance, his eye was caught by a faint blue glow coming off something in the bay. "Anybody know what that is over there?" he asked.

"It's some barge that showed up this morning. No one knows where it came from."

"A large barge with a radio antenna tower on it, from what I hear."

"I saw it from my window this morning. It has a radio antenna on it with a big blue light at the top."

"It's just been floating out there. Blinking."

"It's looks rusty and homemade. Cobbled together by some amateurs."

"Drunken amateurs by the look of it. The tower isn't even straight. Probably won't last the night before it falls over."

"Can't imagine it is transmitting anything but gibberish."

The Protagonist thought back to his earlier conversation with the priest— "It's pretty obvious that they are building something."

"Building what?" the Protagonist had asked.

"They're building a distress beacon, a hotline, I don't know, some kind of shortwave radio transmitter, but one directly connected to God," the priest had replied. "They're trying to get his attention, sending an S.O.S. Trying to get God to remember we are still here."

The Protagonist suddenly rose from the table. His friends had retreated to the safety of their unresolvable argument. Beside a pile of dirty plates, the scientist's dissertation still lay on the table, unread and now stained with a coffee ring and some ketchup. "I've got to go," the Protagonist said. His companions, so engrossed in their debate, failed to even acknowledge his departure.

As he hurried his way through the diner, his exit was momentarily blocked by several paramedics wheeling a person under sheet out of the front door. But once outside, he buttoned up his overcoat and began walking expeditiously in the direction of the harbor.

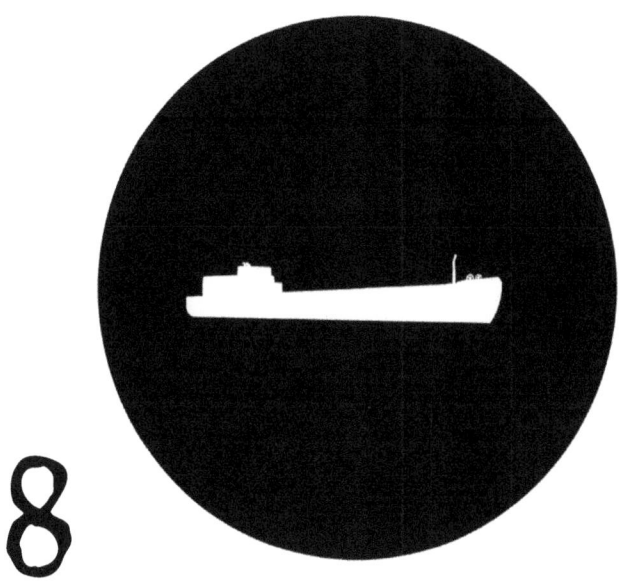

8

For the first time that evening, perhaps for the first time in a long time, the Protagonist's steps had some semblance of purpose. He hurried down a wide, treelined boulevard that lazily descended from the city's highlands all the way to the harbor. The boulevard was long and straight, and from his vantage point he could see across many city blocks and intersections stretching down to the quay on the water's edge. Beyond that was the unlit blackness of the bay, and then beyond that lights twinkled in the distance, sloping uphill on the other side of the city. Little by little, the fog lifted, but some disquieting thing stayed behind in the streets. A headwind arose, and grew stronger as the Protagonist descended towards sea level. He pulled the collar of his coat tight against his throat, and squinted his eyes against the onrushing wind and dust.

Once, this street had been host to numerous parades, but it had been so long since there'd been a parade. Through his narrowed eyes, the Protagonist saw the memory of his younger self sitting expectantly on the boulevard's curb. With a wide grin on his tiny face, the child's fists pumped up and down as an otherwise invisible procession of marching bands and triumphant soldiers, interspersed with exotic animals and typhonic beasts strode past. The Protagonist was sure that he had attended parades long ago, but he couldn't remember the specific details. As the wind died down and his eyes opened fully once again, the child was gone. He continued onward towards the bay.

He began to hear sounds emanating from some blocks further ahead. Faint and indistinct at first, they took on the characteristics of screams as he came closer. Then other, softer sounds began to bubble forth into the night air; shrieks of laughter and festive bells and what could have been the clacking of a train crossing a wooden trestle. After a time, the Protagonist arrived at an intersection that led to the source of the noise– a travelling carnival had set down in a vacant lot on a nearby side street. From behind a hastily-assembled, tattered, canvas fence, the colorful crown of a merry-go-round could be seen twirling. A calliope continually repeated the refrain of a melody originally written about gladiators. Couples and families could be seen exiting the main gate; arms laden with bright balloons, and oversized stuffed animals, and greasy bags of popcorn. Colorful lights blinked on and off, and the indulgent aroma of grilled meats permeated the Protagonist's nostrils. Fireworks suddenly began bursting in the sky overhead.

    He hesitated for a moment, debating whether he should abandon his goal and join the celebration. The jubilant sights, sounds, and smells of the carnival were enticing, but he looked closely at the smiling, unfamiliar faces of the carnival-goers. They were not his tribe. To them, he would always be a stranger, an outsider, someone to be eyed with wary suspicion. He quickly concluded that wandering silently through such a joyful setting would only serve to make him feel even more alone and isolated. He could walk among the carnival-goers, but he could never walk with them, never be one of them. The Protagonist understood that he was only ever able to define himself in terms of what he was not– he was not a lover, he was not a co-worker, he was not a brother-in-arms, he was not a parishioner, he was not a comrade. He was not a carnival-goer. His journey tonight had driven home the fact that none of those terms defined him. Was he a hero or a villain? A loyalist or a revolutionary? A failure or a success? Those terms only had meaning in relation to some zero-point he could not demarcate. He certainly existed, he was sure of that much, yet he possessed no milestone or origin point to anchor that existence to, and so he remained undefined, and in a sense, unreal.

He turned his back to the fireworks and jubilation and continued on his mission towards the harbor. As he walked, the sounds of the carnival receded into silence. First the calliope faded away, then the shrieks of laughter and festive bells and the clacking of a rollercoaster crossing a wooden trestle, until all that could still be heard were the faint and indistinct sounds of screams.

The Protagonist rubbed his hands together as he walked, partially in an attempt to warm himself, but also partially to feel skin against skin, to reassure himself that he possessed actual physical form. Eventually, he reached the end of the boulevard where a long, concrete walk ran parallel to the shore. Above him hung a large billboard depicting the cartoonish face of a small child bearing an impossibly huge grin. He stood leaning against an anodized metal balustrade that prevented the unwary from stumbling off the concrete walk and falling onto the sand below. In the middle of the harbor, a large barge was indeed anchored. It appeared to be shoddily constructed, possibly from pieces scavenged from a collection of other boats. Several spotlights danced erratically from both bow and stern. Their beams pierced the darkness of the bay, yet only allowed the hull to be viewed in discrete segments as they swung across the deck. No markings were present to identify the ship, or its home port, although someone had sloppily scrawled the words "Urim & Thummim" in dark spray paint across the side of the hull. The main deck appeared to be piled high with detritus and scrap metal, which remained dimly illuminated by an ever-changing faint blue glow that seemed to dart from between the heaps. Towering high over the improvised vessel was what appeared to be a tall radio antenna. It seemingly stretched infinitely high into the clear night sky. The Protagonist hoped for answers.

He swung his legs around and jumped down over the balustrade onto the thin beach that separated the sea from the barrier wall. He landed right in front of an Arab man with a determined and angry face. The two looked at each other cautiously, and the Arab fidgeted with an unseen object hidden in his jacket pocket. "I'm sorry, I didn't see you there below me, it's dark," said the Protagonist. The Arab stared at him for a second with fiery eyes, but ultimately proceeded onward without response.

The Protagonist began walking the shore in the opposite direction from the Arab, searching for a way to get closer to the barge. Long-forgotten anti-ship fortifications remained emplaced on the beach, now covered in incomprehensible graffiti, slowing rusting and sinking into the sand. The sea was too choppy and the weather far too cold to consider swimming. He stepped gingerly amongst broken shells and clumps of rotting seaweed. Ahead of him, the beach receded into impenetrable darkness. He turned and debated going in the direction the Arab was headed in hopes of finding a dock or a ferryman willing to take him, but from that direction he suddenly heard a single gunshot ring out in the night. Then, seconds later, four more gunshots in rapid succession. The Protagonist quickly decided to pursue the path he was already on, and hurried down the dark spit of sand away from whatever violence lay behind him.

After a time, he came upon a small rowboat that had been dragged ashore and left abandoned. It was hardly larger than a canoe, but it looked seaworthy enough to get him to the barge. A set of oars lay conveniently half-buried next to the keel. Surreptitiously, the Protagonist looked around for signs of the boat's owner, but not a soul was around. He reasoned that as long as he returned the boat before sunrise, the owner would never notice if he borrowed it. He grabbed the cold, metal bow and started to push it into the water. His hands ran across a sticker that some joker had attached to the hull. It read, "Warning: This Object Does Not Exist," which the Protagonist found humorous considering how heavy he found the boat to be. But he managed to get it deep enough into the tide that it began floating. He splashed his way into the boat with the oars and set out rowing towards the barge.

The Protagonist had little experience piloting boats, and the sea was dark and violent, so progress was slow and meandering. Several times, waves of ice-cold water splashed over the gunwales and onto his pants. He began to shiver forcefully. As the spotlights' beams swept in arcs across the bay, he could catch momentary glimpses of other small boats, containing other pilgrims, also struggling to cross the dark water towards the barge. He continued to row. He bobbed up and down as the waves threatened to overturn his small boat, but the barge seemed eerily immobile and unaffected by the turbulence surrounding it.

This was crazy, the Protagonist thought to himself. He might very well meet his end in these rough seas. If a book was ever written about his life, this would certainly have to be the climactic chapter. He remembered the woman he'd met earlier, Simone; she had told him she was writing a book. There was a chance, a small chance, that it would include some fictionalized version of her encounter with him tonight. And maybe her book would become a best-seller. If so, he would live on in the minds of future generations. But, he realized with some disappointment that Simone had no knowledge of what he was doing right now, or what might await him on the strange barge. There was no possibility that she would include his boat trip in her memoire. She barely knew him at all, so even if she did add him as a character, he was certain to be a completely different person. He would forever be remembered as someone that he was not. The victories and struggles of his own life completely overwritten by a crude fictionalization. And he was powerless to stop it.

Afraid, he buoyed his spirits with the words of that crazed soldier from his dream; he would either make it safely to the barge, or capsize and drown. But if he drowned, he would no longer be here to observe himself drowned, so the only possible result he could ever observe was success. So he rowed onward.

He approached the barge nearest its prow. Several skiffs, canoes, makeshift rafts, and even what looked like a surfboard, sat empty and abandoned in the water, being thrown about by the waves. From high above, an unseen hand tossed a rope ladder off the deck. It unfurled as it fell, each rung clanging against the metal hull in turn. The Protagonist reached out and grabbed it, and climbed upwards out of his boat. The ladder swayed in the wind as he ascended, several times causing him to momentarily pause and hold on tightly so as not to fall. He made the mistake of looking down, just once, and saw the water now far below him, almost enticing him to release his grip and plunge into the churning blackness. But he steadily continued upwards.

As he reached the top, he was helped on board by an Erelim patiently waiting under a hand-painted wooden sign that read, "KETER." The Erelim grabbed his hand and began guiding him across the deck. The creature tugged at his sleeve and its touch left an oily residue that faintly glowed.

He had never seen an Erelim up close before. It was, of course, impossible to look at it directly. He could only see it as one sees something out of the corner of one's eye. It was organic, and alien, and clockwork, and angelic all at once, and continually transformed and oscillated between its phases– an onslaught of kaleidoscopic shapes that never quite coalesced into a singular form. Their faces were jumbled, abstracted, and leaking colored light. And they sang.

The Erelim steered him through what felt like an infinite maze of corridors, haphazardly meandering between rickety wooden crates, mounds of jagged scrap metal, and heaps of random junk. They moved quickly; forwards and backwards, right and left, down and up, through light and through darkness, through good and through evil. At several intersections, the Protagonist could see other Erelim hastily dragging along other confused pilgrims behind them down different paths. All the while, the self-transforming machine elves were singing in unison in a hyperdimensional adamic language that seemed to say, "Welcome, we're so glad you're here."

As the Protagonist and his guide moved from clearing to clearing, he began to recognize items from his past mixed in among the detritus cluttering the deck. Something about that baby blanket seemed eerily familiar to him, a pile of comic books that he half-remembered reading. A pennant from a little-league team he might have played on. Nothing was identifiable enough to be sure, and the Erelim moved too swiftly for the Protagonist to pause and contemplate the items as they rushed by. However, he began to wonder about the items he didn't recognize. Were those on the barge because of random chance, for the benefit of other pilgrims, or could those things also be part of the Protagonist's own past, albeit from a time that he had erased from his own mind? A heap of empty liquor bottles. The rusted shell of a car that had once been in a terrible crash. A pistol whose barrel still contained a wisp of smoke. Were these things evidence of something terrible that he willfully chose to not remember? The Protagonist wanted to believe that he was a good person, but perhaps that was only a fiction of selective memory.

He did not have time to contemplate this idea, as soon the Protagonist and his guide arrived at the final clearing, which was located at the very the rear of the main deck, and directly underneath the massive radio antenna that could be seen from shore. From this vantage point, it was difficult to tell where the antenna ended. It rose up, up into the sky, seemingly infinitely high. It looked as one might imagine an antenna would look if it were rising not upwards in space, but perhaps rising through some indefinable fourth dimension, although that might have just been an optical illusion created by judicious sizing of each segment of the antenna. When the Protagonist looked back down, the Erelim that had been guiding him was gone.

He was left at the end of a line of people queuing patiently. "Why do you think they built this way out here on this barge?" he asked a woman standing in front of him, to pass the time. "Wouldn't it have been easier if they put it on the land somewhere?"

"It has to be here. Exactly here. The transmitter only works if it is located at the exact geometric center of the universe, and that turned out to be out here right in the middle of the bay," she replied.

"How do you know that this is the exact center of the universe?"

"Look for yourself." She pointed at a mechanism located underneath the antenna. A rotating platform containing an incandescent bulb with several mirrors spinning around its axis, slowly and unchangingly.

"Oh, I see." said the Protagonist.

A number of desks and tables had been indiscriminately arranged on the deck around the base of the antenna. A telephone had been placed on each one. From the phones, wires ran across the deck, each plugged into a large mechanism covered in gears and vacuum tubes and innumerable flashing lights, some of which spelled out the word, "**MALKUTH**." The mechanism was in turn connected to the antenna by a large cable that pulsed like an artery. At each of these stations sat a pilgrim. Right in front of the Protagonist, an older lady was clutching her phone to her ear and crying hysterically. Next to her, a young, angry man was shouting and violently slamming his receiver onto his desk. A few stations down, another woman could be heard begging, "Please! Please! Don't leave me here!" over and over again into her handset, her face puffy and dripping with tears and mucous. A man with a wandering eye ended his conversation, carefully placed his handset back on its base, calmly stood up from his station, and walked over to the gunwales. He turned towards the Protagonist, and with his arms outstretched, he allowed himself to fall backwards over the railing into the icy water below. No one tried to stop him. An Erelim busy repairing some wiring above paused, peered down at the Protagonist, and with its infinite eyes offered the now-empty seat to him.

    The Protagonist cautiously sat down at the old, metallic desk. The seat of the chair was still warm from the previous occupant. The furniture had clearly once been in an office somewhere, and some now-anonymous worker had long ago scraped their initials into the surface of the desk. On a dark green blotter that was covered in scribbles and math sums, rested a rotary phone of black bakelite. A small white light on the phone blinked on and off. The Protagonist stared at it for a few moments without moving. A woman ran past him screaming with rage and terror, close enough that her perfume caught his attention as she flew by. The small light on the phone continued to blink on and off. Two nearby men became involved in a fistfight, with several Erelim struggling unsuccessfully to pull them apart. The Protagonist could not bring himself to pick up the receiver. Instead, he distracted himself by opening the drawers of the desk. Most were empty, but one contained an addressed, yet unsent, letter that had undoubtedly been left behind long ago when the desk was surplused to whatever junkyard the Erelim had acquired it from. The paper was now yellowed with age. The Protagonist was curious of the contents of the letter, and wondered if it was left unsent due to simple oversight or willful hesitation on the part of the writer. He considered taking the letter and bringing it to its intended recipient, but decided against doing that. Whatever words the letter contained, the time had long since passed for them to possibly bring any comfort to its reader.

    The line behind him appeared to be becoming impatient. Overcoming his qualms, he reached over and picked up the handset and put the receiver to his ear. "Hello?" he asked sheepishly. There was nothing but silence on the other end. Less than silence, it was almost as if a vacuum was hungrily pulling sound through the receiver to fill an endless void at the other end of the line.

It wasn't until that moment that he considered all the things that he could say. Pleas, entreaties, threats, and logical arguments all jumbled competitively through his mind. He gazed up at the impossibly tall antenna he was connected to, and wondered who or what could be at the other end. The Protagonist was so unsure of himself and his past, so confused as how things came to be the way they were in this entropic city he lived in, how could he relate to whatever was listening up there? Could there be some perfected, four-dimensional version of his soul hovering above, waiting to hear from him? He imagined the children he'd seen at the arcade earlier, and imagined how they would react if a tiny pixilated warrior suddenly turned to them and asked for comfort and succor through the screen. Would they understand? Would they even listen? Could they help even if they wanted to? Could anything– even a singular, omnipotent entity existing in all possible higher dimensions, actually twist reality in the Protagonist's favor here in the present? Or had the universe already been superdetermined from its inception? Inanimate nature running on behind-the-scenes clockwork. Cause precipitating effect precipitating secondary causes and secondary effects, like balls zooming around a pool table, all following paths that were inexorably predetermined from the moment the cue ball was first struck. If that were the case, then in the entire history of the universe, only that single, initiating cause mattered, and whatever that event was, it was by this point forever unalterable in the distant past. Asking for help now would be as pointless as reaching your hand out to grab a ledge well after you've tumbled off the cliff.

"Am I... am I even real?" was the question he eventually settled upon asking. He turned to look directly at the reader, but no matter which direction he cast his eyes, he could not see up into the higher dimensions. Straining to see God is like straining to look at the back of your own head. You know for certain it is close by, but it can never be in view. The phone gave no obvious response to his question. But was a response even possible? Perhaps information can only travel in one direction through the dimensions? From lower-order to higher. A fictional character in a book can easily communicate to a reader, but no matter how loud they shout, the reader can never respond in a way the character can perceive. Even if some entity up there could hear him, and was sympathetic to his cause, it would not be able to offer him anything but silence.

He came to the conclusion that he had been searching for something he could never find. Whether or not there was was some underlying eternal and objective meaning to existence was an unresolvable question, since the fundamental laws of the universe prevented anyone living inside of it from ever knowing what that meaning could possibly be. It didn't matter if this city was a real place, or a fictional place, or an allegorical hell completely abandoned by an uncaring creator. But the city didn't require a deeper meaning to exist. It was what it was. He was here. That is all.

The Protagonist calmly placed the receiver back on the base without saying another word. He stood and looked around at the desperate mass of lonely and despondent people who had gathered to plead for some ray of hope that could soothe the pain of their miserable and pointless existence. However 'real' the

Protagonist was, were they not all as equally real? They seemed to be. At least their suffering seemed to be real.

He remembered a parable: A man and a child were walking along a beach that was covered in struggling starfish, tossed out of the ocean by the tides. The boy picked up one starfish and threw it back into the safety of the water. "Do you realize there are miles of miles of beach and thousands of starfish?" said the father, "You can't make any appreciable difference."

"Maybe not," replied the boy, "but at least I made a difference to that one."

The Protagonist took a deep breath and prayed that God would give him enough time and enough sense and strength to be able to tell people what he knew, so they'd know what he knew and not despair so much. He climbed up onto the desk. "Why are we all so alone here?" he shouted to the crowd. "I don't where we are, I don't know why we are here, or what any of this means. But no matter how terrible it is, this is what we have... this is all we have. Can we not make the best of it? Why do we each choose solitary sorrow? What is hell? I maintain that it is the suffering of being unable to love. But we can love if we want to love. No one is stopping us except ourselves. We don't need to beg for salvation. We are all right here, aren't we able to love each other? We don't have to be alone."

No one turned to face him. No one listened. No one seemed to have been paying attention to his words. Everyone was lost in their own independent miasma of despair. It was as if they couldn't even see one another; like characters from two different movies simultaneously projected onto the same screen. Each cry of anger and wail of desperation fell on deaf ears. Not just on the ears of whatever was on the other end of the Erelim's contraption, but on the ears of the other supplicants milling about on the deck. Not a single starfish was saved, thought the Protagonist. A communication unfortunately takes two people. He just didn't have the skill to explain his revelation in a way that anyone could understand. His Venn diagram would never intersect with theirs. We are each forever trapped in solitary confinement in the prison behind our own eyes, he thought. They'd have to figure it out for themselves.

He got down off the desk. Two pilgrims rushed to take his place and began scuffling over control of the black bakelite phone. The

Protagonist just walked away in despair. Wandering the serpentine corridors of trash that cluttered the deck, he made one last feeble attempt at connection. He came across a woman leaning against the rusted-out shell of an old car, sobbing quietly. The Protagonist hugged her. She jumped back and slapped him in the face, "don't touch me you creep!" she yelled.

He retraced the path that had brought him to the antenna, this time without the help of an Erelim. He lost his way several times, but he eventually found the rope ladder that led to his skiff. As the spotlights swept across the bay in great arc, he could see more people approaching the barge in their tiny boats. He felt sorry for them.

9

The borrowed skiff still bobbed in the surf below the rope ladder. The Protagonist lowered himself back down from the barge's deck. During his absence, a few inches of frigid water had splashed into the boat, and he found himself having to brace his feet up on the transom to avoid getting soaked. Using one of the oars, he pushed off from the massive hull and began floating away. As he travelled farther and further from the barge, it receded into the distance and appeared to shrink smaller and smaller. But perhaps the barge remained unchanged, and it was really the Protagonist himself that was getting smaller and smaller, and lonelier and lonelier, as he rushed away from the lights and the assistance of the Erelim.

He aimed the boat for lights emanating from the shore where he had launched himself. For a moment, he thought he could hear an oboe, droning an A note, coming from the direction he was headed. He rowed faster, hoping to get close enough to tune himself to whomever was waiting for him on the beach. But even after several minutes of rowing, the lights on the shore seemed to be growing smaller and smaller as well.

He was caught in the outgoing tide rushing from the bay to the deep sea. He beat on against the current, but was borne ceaseless away from his destination. No matter how hard he tried, the water dragged him away faster than he could row. As the distance between himself and the shore inexorably increased, the Protagonist conceded that it was now something forever unreachable in his past. Even the blue smudge the Erelim had left on his sleeve had faded away. He could no more return to the barge or the shore than he could return to the events that happened earlier in the evening at the bar, or the church, or the library. His future wasn't measured in a tick on a clock, but in his inevitable velocity in the direction of the skiff's bow.

An icy fog started to roll in, and one by one the lights of the city's shoreline dimmed and faded away. In turn, even the large barge and its bright spotlights slowly vanished from view completely as they too became obscured in the mist. No longer having an obvious reference point to navigate from, the Protagonist became a bit disoriented and unable to determine which direction led to the beach. A steady wind blew him along with the current until he concluded that he was so lost there was little point in continuing to row in any particular direction. He set the oars back in the boat and huddled for warmth, allowing the boat to continue along whatever predetermined course it was on through this great sea of blackness.

He closed his eyes to protect against a sudden gust, and when he opened them again, he could see no lights, could hear no sounds. In every direction, all that existed was a white blanket of opaque fog, making it appear to the Protagonist that he was inside of a large ping pong ball. The sea had become unusually calm, with no waves or whitecaps to break up the darkness. He peered over the edge of the skiff into the water. It was just an unfathomable, bottomless blackness. Perhaps somewhere down in the depths was a fish or a rusted anchor, but there was no way to tell. From the surface, it seemed to be limitless darkness.

He began to imagine that this is what nothingness was like. A sheer emptiness consisting of nothing except for impenetrable blackness; no lights, no sounds, no particles, no energy. With no external reference, it was impossible to even tell whether time itself was passing or not. He enjoyed a moment of quiet reflection and pondered the nature of eternity. But he soon realized that there was one thing disrupting the purity of this vast emptiness—himself. He was a something. And since he was an observer intruding into the nothingness, the emptiness surrounding him, as empty as it was, could never be considered a "true nothingness." A true nothingness would have to be completely invisible as, by definition, no observer can ever be there to perceive the nothing without being a something to disrupt the nothing. If that was the case, then true nothingness is not defined as a "0," it is a "?." Without an observer to check, it is not possible to ever say for sure what is inside the true nothing. And if it is impossible, by definition, to know what's inside of a true nothing, then wouldn't anything and everything be equally likely to be inside? Every combination of every possible object in every possible configuration was encompassed in the definition of "?" wasn't it? True nothingness is not empty, it is actually a giant, amorphous blob of everything all at once. Until some outside observer looks inside the box, it could be said to contain every possible thing; everything and every thing and nothing all at once. Perhaps this entire city was just a random manifestation of some undefinable amorphous blob inside a giant box no one happened to be looking into at the present time. And if that external entity, which existed outside the universe, opened the box and peered in, the "?" would collapse back into a "0" and the city would cease to exist.

    The Protagonist was rocked as the skiff suddenly ran aground. He was thrown off his seat into the frigid water at the bottom of the boat. He arose to find himself and the boat lodged upon a rocky shore. It wasn't the same beach he had departed from, but at least it was dry land. He climbed out of the boat and dragged it up out of the tide, where he left it. Then he scrambled up the riprap lining the shore and hopped over a low stone wall. He found himself in a small grove of trees, and pushing his way through the brambles and undergrowth, he emerged into a seemingly endless graveyard. There were a few lights to guide his way, and he soon found a path that might lead back to a gate leading to a city street.

The tree-lined path meandered in a circuitous route past groves of tombstones. They rose from the ground in symmetrical patches, as if they were crops that were almost ready for harvest. A few gaudy monuments were scattered in between long, straight rows of modest, identical headstones. Some were muddied and overgrown with brown grass, others showed signs of having been tidied at some point in the not-so-distant past. Dead flowers and decayed wreaths littered the ground. The roots of a large tree had evidently grown and half-upturned a nearby gravestone whose epithet was partially obscured by moss. The upper-section of the ancient and eroded stone had already cracked and fallen off. What remained was left teetering precariously, slanted at a 45-degree angle. Someday soon it would fall over completely. The Protagonist felt a hint of sadness for the poor unfortunate soul who was buried in this inopportune location. Was there anyone left alive in this city who even remembered the person who was interned here? He tried to read the stone, but the upper part, the part containing the name, was crumbled and lost. The only part that wasn't too weathered to make out clearly were the words,

her suffering is mercifully concluded

He sat on a bench next to the tree and kept the tilting tombstone company for a moment. "Hello," he said to it. "I can't tell what your name is, so I'm just going to make one up." He did so, and found himself imagining other details about the interred person's life to fill the gaps. "Let's see, how did you end up in this sorry state?" he asked. "Looks like you were buried here... I'm going to guess seventy-five years ago. No, a hundred," he said, based on the eroded condition of the stone. "I will assume that you were married and had children. But then you lost your husband to the war, and your children to a disease that would have been easily curable today. That's pretty tragic, I'm sorry to hear that." He tried to balance that thought by imagining some happy days in her life– as a child blowing out candles on a birthday cake, as a teen sitting in warm summer parks making eyes at a special boy, a vision of rice thrown on a wedding day. "But at the end, it was just you, alone and forgotten as a dowager, surviving in a set of small, cold rooms on a meager pension." He imagined that after she passed, her neighbors, who never bothered to know her while she still breathed, chipped in out of guilt to buy this small plot for her final rest.

The Protagonist knew that this tale was completely fictional, and it would only be coincidence if any part of it matched up with the deceased's actual life. But it was as believable as any other version. As far as the Protagonist knew, there might not even be anyone buried in this plot at all. He bent down and touched the soil with his hand. Six feet underneath him was a box that could never be opened, filled with facts that could never be known, about a person he would never meet. The only way to be certain about anything related to this corpse was to travel back in time to when they still lived. But the current of time is one-direction. It was impossible to peer inside that box; the person buried here was forever more a "?," and by definition they were now just a superposition of anything and anyone and everything that they could have possibly been, all at the same time. There was no longer any functional difference between the actual person that had once lived, and the infinite number of fictional versions of the person that any passerby cared to imagine.

The Protagonist extrapolated to note that this effect was observable, even before death. As he walked the streets of the city earlier tonight, he passed by many strange faces that never interacted with him before and would never again. In their eyes, his entire past was a "?." These anonymous strangers could make up any story about him and it would be as true as any other, wouldn't it? It was impossible for anyone to know anything about the Protagonist's childhood, whether he fought in a war, or worked in a factory. By this particular point in time, these events were just stories, unverifiable. In that way, even though he still lived, the Protagonist was as fictional as the person whose grave he currently sat in front of.

The universe is just a set of lies we tell ourselves to feel like we matter.

It began raining heavily, but the Protagonist was already as wet as he could possibly get from his time in the boat, so he had little motivation to seek shelter. Soon, a rivulet of rainwater formed on the path. He watched as the water flowed from higher ground, past his feet, down the slight gradient, and drained into a sewer grate. Individual leaves bobbed and floated, carried along by the current. On occasion, two leaves would bump into each other for a second, then separate to pursue their individual paths once again. They couldn't go back upstream, their only interactions with each other were fleeting and pointless, and the end of their journeys were inevitable. The Protagonist saw similarities between himself and the leaves. He wished he could hold on to someone and never let them go. He wished he could hold on to a moment and never let it slip by. He wished he could stop the relentless push that pressed him forward towards an inevitable future where everything increases in entropy; decaying, withering, and falling apart. But, like the leaves, he was being involuntarily pulled through time by inescapable force. What was the nature of that force? Was God the singularity at the end of time, inexorably pulling us towards its domain in the far future? Or was it something as meaningless and farcical as a cosmic sewer grate? There was no way to know until you finally arrived at the end of time, and by that point it was too late.

    He looked up and noticed that beyond the tree, some distance off the path, a lone lamppost illuminated a small section of the graveyard. The Protagonist found himself drawn through the rows of stones towards the light. He stumbled over unseen obstacles in the dark underbrush and stubbed a toe more than once, but he arrived at the lamppost that had beckoned to him. Beneath the light were a number of fresher graves. So fresh in fact that the stones hadn't been carved yet. They were totally blank. There seemed a certain familiarity to them, but he couldn't quite recall how he knew them. It was really impossible to be sure of anything about any of the people interred in this grove. The Protagonist had a disturbing thought, if anyone could be buried here, then maybe the grave he was standing on was his own? He realized that didn't make sense, as he was clearly here on the surface, but the infinite set of things included in the "?" would encompass both the set of everything that made sense, and the set of everything that didn't. In some uncollapsed part of the probability wave function, he was the corpse buried under his feet. And not just this one grave, but all of these graves. Not just in this grove, but throughout the entire cemetery. Not just this cemetery, but all cemeteries everywhere in the universe. His eyes scanned row after row of tombstones, stretching as far as his eye could see; each one containing himself, or some probabilistic version of himself, that had made a slightly different set of choices in life that resulted in a different collapse of the probability wave function. A thousand alternate paths. A thousand tragic accidents. A thousand gruesome diseases. A thousand lonely suicides. All paths as equally true, as equally fictional, as the one that led him to be standing here, lost and alone in the rain.

In the distance, a flash of lightning crossed the sky, and the lamp above him flickered momentarily due to some disruption in the power line. In that brief instance, probably due to some trick of the light, the Protagonist glimpsed names etched across the stones in the grove. They were his own. He backed away from the stone he was standing in front of in terror, unsettled at the idea of standing upon his own grave. He turned and ran, and almost immediately felt himself tumbling through space.

He had a vision of himself leaping from a balcony and hurtling past windows and awnings onto the sidewalk below. As he lay crushed and deflated on the ground, he could see the feet of a couple with better places to be gingerly walking past.

He had a vision of himself alone and tortured in a darkened and unheated room. Only a flickering candle provides him with enough light to load the pistol.

He had a vision of himself touring a factory's production floor. A large machine violently stamps metal in front of him. He fidgets with his necktie, and imagines what would happen should it get caught in the gears. The idea delights him more than he expected it would.

He had a vision of himself, swinging from a rope tied about his neck, wishing he had jumped from a slightly greater height to save himself the suffering of strangulation.

He had a vision of himself lying on pavement, too dope sick to sit up, as lines of fashionable young men and woman filed past, incapable of even noticing his suffering.

He had a vision of himself crossing a horrific no-man's land, rifle in hand, inhuman war cries screaming from his lips, then suddenly flying through the air, ripped to pieces from a volley of grapeshot.

He had a vision of not being able to breathe. Everything fading to black as the cries of helpless restaurant patrons filled his ears.

He had a vision of extreme hopelessness and nihilism as he swirled and sank deeper and deeper through dark and frigid water. His last thought was a hope that the "0" would revert to a "?" on account of his no longer being an observer to this universe. No one would ever know of his sacrifice.

He awoke to a throbbing pain in the back of his head. He slowly opened his eyes and found himself lying in the mud at the bottom of a deep hole. He remained motionless for a few moments, calmly watching the light from the nearby lamppost reflect in the raindrops as they fell down on him, and he despaired.

He felt his body fading into something as anonymous and as fictional as the rest of the poor souls interred in this dreadful place. He could think of no proof that any of the events of his life had even happened at all. Perhaps it was all just delusion. Was he even actually here, at the bottom of this open grave, or was he simply a random collection of atoms somewhere in the cosmos that spontaneously came together in a pattern that, for an instant, mimicked a self-aware brain. One replete with delusions of a past that never happened? A statistical fluctuation that remained intact just long enough to have a single coherent thought or observation, only to then disappear into the vacuum as suddenly as it appeared?

Finding himself at such a low point, no past to cling to, no future to look forward to, now lost down an oubliette; he descended into a solitude so frightful that he contemplated suicide. What held him back was the idea that no one, absolutely no one, would be moved by his death; that he would be even more alone in death than in life. Suicide is a confession that the state of being dead is somehow more meaningful than the state of being alive. Yet, the pointlessness and absurdity of life could not be solved by death, which is itself an equally pointless and absurd state of being. There was no functional difference between the two. Existence being just a game we are all forced against our will to play. A game we can't win, we can't tie, and we can't even decline to play.

The Protagonist reached the conclusion that while life was not worth living, death was also not worth dying, and the meaninglessness of existence could not be the determining factor in how one must proceed. The past was by definition unobservable, forever beyond reach, and the future existed as nothing more than an uncollapsed probability of all that might possibly happen. Neither had any bearing on the fleeting moment in time known as "now." Any action one might take in any particular instant was as equally valid as any other. No right or wrong choices existed. No mistakes could be made because the test would forever remain ungraded. The Protagonist felt a great weight lift off of him.

He sat up and rubbed his head with hand. The back of his hair was sticky with blood from the rock he had fallen upon. The pit he had fallen into in was six feet deep with squared-off walls. He rose to his feet and clawed his way back to the surface. With a dirty finger, he wrote his name on the blank tombstone above the open hole. He brushed the muck off of his overcoat as best he could and found his pocket filled with dirt. He withdrew a handful and tossed it into his grave and then continued on his way.

He returned to the tilting tombstone he had visited earlier, and knelt beside it. "No," the Protagonist whispered to it. "I retract that entire story about your life. I couldn't help you with any of your troubles while you walked this earth. But I can overwrite them now." He made up a story in his mind about the person below him. A wonderful story about a wonderful life, filled with excitement and joy and meaning. The words "her suffering is mercifully concluded" on the tombstone were a final ironic joke made by her loved ones.

"You hear that!" he shouted to the heavens. "That is this person's true life story!" He took the heaven's silence as acquiescence.

Feeling good about himself for his noble act, the Protagonist turned to his own past, and imagined himself a happy childhood filled with love, and a life replete with meaning and without trauma. Whatever truth he'd lived before today, it was forevermore unreachable, a "?," and so it could be filled with anything. Why should he continue to suffer in the present for trauma from an unobservable and inherently fungible past?

He arrived at a crossroads in the meandering cemetery path near an elaborate gravestone marked with the name, "Kerr." A large puddle had formed there due to a clogged drain. The Protagonist kicked some debris free and the water began to flow again. He watched the current, and observed that the water didn't flow directly into the sewer in a straight line, but instead swirled around it in a whirlpool. Leaves floating in the puddle circled around faster and faster as they were drawn into the vortex. What if time isn't like a river, the Protagonist thought to himself, but like a whirlpool? In a river, everything upstream is forever more out of reach, but the same isn't true of a whirlpool. While it is true that you can never go counterclockwise against the current, if you wait patiently, the clockwise rotation will inevitably return you to the same place you once had been, over and over again. Could it be that falling far enough into future brings you back to the past? Maybe, if he waited patiently, the inescapable current of time would complete a rotation and return him to where he'd been before. Each revolution tracing the same path again and again. Each revolution falling a little farther down towards the center. Each circuit, a slight bit more compact. And with each rotation, each floating leaf grows closer to the other leaves also caught in the vortex. Each revolution bringing him a little closer to the God that was the singularity that existed at the end of time.

Maybe the next cycle would be different. Maybe he wouldn't be so alone. Maybe he would be able to finally grab on to some person, some hope, some meaning, some tribe, as it crossed paths with him in the tightening gyre. And if not in this revolution, maybe in the next, or the next after that, or the next after that...

He would have to find something to occupy himself with in the meantime, while he waited to complete his circuit around the vortex. He reached the front gate of the cemetery and exited back onto the streets of the city. The sidewalk in front of him was stained dark with water. Small droplets on his glasses turned the streetlights into astigmatic pinwheels in his eyes.

He walked at random, calm and empty, under a wasted sky.

www.ingramcontent.com/pod-product-compliance
Lightning Source LLC
LaVergne TN
LVHW010307070426
835512LV00029B/3497